THE BUSINESS OF
TIMESHARES

www.amplifypublishing.com

The Business of Timeshares:
Uncovering the Peaks and Valleys of an Enigmatic Industry

For more information, please contact:
Amplify Publishing, an imprint of Mascot Books
620 Herndon Parkway, Suite 320
Herndon, VA 20170
info@amplifypublishing.com

Library of Congress Control Number: 2021913200

CPSIA Code: PRFRE0122A

ISBN-13: 978-1-64543-642-3

Printed in Canada

This book is dedicated to all those who've been asked to agree (or disagree) with the terms and conditions of a product or service they are about to purchase.

In most cases they are delivered through smart, efficient technology whereupon a buyer may quickly agree by activating a prompt once they have scrolled down and ostensibly read thousands of words of boilerplate fine print. There is a mild degree of intimidation involved.

Understandably, it's said to protect both the buyer and seller. But you can be sure it's the interests of the seller that are paramount; if delivered in person, it's that which drives an otherwise innocent administrative processor to stare calmly over their desk at the buyer as if to imply that everything awaits their response.

Virtually all buyers, for their own reasons—including this one—scroll down as far as they must to find the "agree" prompt and quickly activate it, but for this one, still with a mild degree of incongruent efficiency.

Sometimes that response is backed by prior experience with the seller, but far more often it's not.

While the timeshare industry deserves close scrutiny from an unlikely critic, one with experience as real estate investor, financial advisor, and multiple timeshare owner, my purpose here is not to denigrate them. Rather, it's to urge them to become a responsible seller of their product and service by doing, at the very least, what's routinely delivered by other industries to protect their financial interests. And that is to provide adequate disclosure at point of sale to all buyers, regardless of what the industry deems to be their "need" for it. By refusing to do this, there is much more than a mild degree of intimidation involved.

While the industry disagrees, most timeshare buyers need a brief, concise, and easily readable reminder of the basic business characteristics of their purchase.

Enjoy the read!

THE BUSINESS OF
TIMESHARES

UNCOVERING THE PEAKS
AND VALLEYS OF AN
ENIGMATIC INDUSTRY

W.H. CAMPBELL

*REAL ESTATE INVESTOR
AND FINANCIAL ADVISOR*

CONTENTS

Introduction
WHY THIS BOOK?

I have climbed Everest. I have navigated ships through agonizing hours of shallow, inland waterways in a war zone. My brow has dripped sweat as I directed the extraction of a jammed hot round from a five-inch gun barrel before it could blow. I have sold men millions in life insurance policies, and I have breathed life into real estate investments.

I am not a man who backs down from a challenge, and I have faced enough formidable challengers to develop my sights. I can size up an issue and start rallying solutions before most even know a problem exists. I have scaled mountains and skyscrapers to bring you the information in this book because I have faced the conundrum that is the timeshare industry and asked its top management the uncomfortable questions no one else dare, challenging their very business model. When I try to untangle what I've learned about timeshares over the last few years, my findings evoke Winston Churchill's famous description of Russia: "a riddle wrapped in a mystery inside an enigma."

From their inception, timeshares have been sold to consumers as a means of leveraging their vacation dollars. As the pitch goes, buying the hotel with a group of like-minded vacationers is cheaper than renting the room. This economy of scale, conceptually packaged as if the consumer were buying real property, made sense to vacationers, and the idea caught on.

But the word "timeshare" now has pejorative connotations among financial advisors and others, for good (but often shallow) reasons. That's because the industry is, for the most part, selling to the wrong customers in the wrong way and for the wrong reasons. Yet, timeshares *do indeed* have a form of leverage—albeit not as originally sold.

What follows is a story that must be told for two important reasons. The first is to fill a void, as no book presents a balanced view of timeshares for consumers. Even among upscale property developers, outside the industry, little is actually known of timeshare inner workings due to their secretive, insular nature. I'm an experienced real estate investor, financial advisor and multiple timeshare owner—yet, *still* an outsider, and thus, think differently. This book explores the world of timeshares and the desirable leverage that exists for the suitable and well-informed buyer.

The second is to urge the timeshare industry to fundamentally transform itself so that it can be held in greater esteem by the consuming public and their financial advisors. I have found both timeshares and the "supporting industries" to be formidable, entrenched and enslaved to their own coda. They have been doing themselves and the public a disservice by remaining so parochial—part of their modus operandi from the beginning. Real reform is needed.

Many outsiders have demanded reform in the past, yet most have concluded that such efforts are a Sisyphean exercise. Because my experience suggests the existence of a well-coordinated model (replete with self-regulatory provisions and a "consumer protection" façade) which insulates them from serious oversight, it's left to consumers to apply the necessary heat to the timeshare industry.

It brings to mind another quote from the "British

Bulldog": "The truth is incontrovertible, malice may attack it, ignorance may deride it, but in the end, there it is."

In this era of marketing and financial compliance, I'm committed to nudging the industry toward transformation. Purchasing a timeshare should be a serious financial decision for those suitable, not one targeted to anyone with a "heartbeat, credit card, and willingness to hear a presentation." While the existing timeshare business model works for the industry (frankly, as a real estate investor, I would love to be able to operate within the timeshare business model as I see it), it strikes me as fundamentally flawed from a consumer perspective, particularly in its execution. Thus, it should be changed for the good of the buying public. While the information I'll share will benefit countless individuals and families, I believe the timeshare industry and the many symbiotic industries spawning from it can also benefit.

Certain characters are introduced by name on my road to discovery. While names have been changed, each one is a real person within the timeshare industry, staff and senior executives with whom I have either met in person or engaged by phone. All strike me as excellent employees and executives who are loyal, capable, and simply carrying out their assigned duties. Indeed, some are remarkable in their pursuit of excellence. The problems addressed herein are not of their making. Rather, it's the business model and culture within which they work. This book is dedicated to uncovering the peaks and valleys of this enigmatic industry; I introduce these individuals only as they are my own touchpoint and connections to the larger machinery.

Although I've sprinkled some of my correspondence with industry officials ranging from a timeshare sales manager to a corporate manager to senior executives to the chief executive officer of a timeshare parent corporation throughout the book to illustrate my points, the appendices provide all of this communication in sequence without comment—properly redacted, of course, yet retaining the essence of its message. You should consider them essential reading, as, in their original state, they'll give you an even clearer view of the questions even a veteran timeshare owner can have and how eager the industry is to ensure answers are not forthcoming.

Yes, for the right buyer, timeshares may be better than you may think . . . but read this book before buying one!

Chapter 1

AN IDEAL VACATION AT YOUR "HOME AWAY FROM HOME"

My first experience with a timeshare started like a dream on a beautiful fall afternoon. Weeks before, my wife and I had committed to a new life as timeshare owners (whatever that was) at the Old Guard in New York City. Although we weren't entirely clear on the business arrangements, that seemed irrelevant. We knew we could afford the initial cost and ongoing fees, so here we went—we were so excited!

We enjoyed a five-hour drive through some beautiful countryside and into the Lincoln Tunnel to our "new" Midtown Manhattan property. Any remaining misgivings were quickly overtaken by the utter thrill of the arrival. There was something especially joyful about the carefree feeling of valet parking in NYC, with our own staff taking care of bags and every detail of check-in.

We found our suite to be even larger and better appointed than expected, so luxurious that our first thought was, *Why would we ever leave such a place?* But then again, we were in the heart of the Big Apple—so close to everything! For us, it was hard to imagine such easy access to so many world-famous attractions: Carnegie Hall, Broadway, Times Square, Rockefeller Center, Central Park, Fifth Avenue, Lincoln Center for Performing Arts, great restaurants, etc., etc.! It seemed a waste to spend any time inside, let alone sleep. Suffice to say, we were on a high!

That was over twenty years ago; for me, this has never changed. That timeshare truly has become a home away from home, with smiling staff members who now feel like family—most of whom remain on the job to this day. As we've matured and become accustomed to New York, the thrill remains. I love the intensity of the city and its ever-changing skyline.

What are Timeshares?

When you get right down to it, timeshares are essentially a group of people sharing the cost of vacation accommodations—a simple concept with many variations and a surprisingly short and sometimes obfuscated history as drawn from open and widely available sources.

There are several projects that lay claim to the title of the first timeshare, but the most likely is Hapimag, out of Zug, Switzerland. Alexander Nette and Dr. Guido Renggli began Hapimag in 1963 after purchasing a few resort properties in Italy and selling eager travelers "rent-free vacations" in the form of right-to-use shares. Just one year after launching, they invented the first points system, which has become one of the most widely-employed forms of timeshare in the world. (We will take a closer look at that in Chapter Two.) With a portfolio now spanning many countries, Hapimag is still successful and independent, which is quite a feat in a market where the largest timeshare companies are marked with names as recognizable as Disney, Hilton, Hyatt, and Marriott.

The SuperDévoluy ski resort in Le Dévoluy, a commune in the French Alps, became perhaps the first deeded timeshare program when it opened in

1968. Though a huge contribution to the development of the timeshare industry as a whole, even that is overshadowed by its advertising slogan: "Why rent the room when it's cheaper to buy the hotel?" It's a pitch that captured—and has continued to capture—the attention of audiences ever since.

Though the first American timeshare, the Hilton Hale Kaanapali in Maui, was built in 1965 and launched a series of other projects in Hawaii, it took nearly a decade for any developers to latch onto the concept in the contiguous forty-eight. When Innisfree Companies and Hyatt opened Brockway Springs in Lake Tahoe, California in 1973, they did more than just introduce timeshares to the mainland. They, in fact, were the first to call their project a "timeshare"—a term borrowed from the burgeoning tech industry. In the face of an economic recession, this branding captured the attention of developers, financiers, and consumers alike. The following year, the Sanibel Beach Club in Florida became the first ownership resort specifically built to be a timeshare; all thirty-one units sold out in the first eighteen months, spurring the development of more timeshare projects and the conversion of many vacation homes to a timeshare model.

The concept of "timeshares" has grown over the decades. The umbrella now covers traditional deeded timeshares, fractional ownerships, private residence clubs, destination clubs, and points clubs; arguably, it can even include campground memberships and the "condo hotel" concept. Still, the basic premise of timeshare is simple: you and a group of other people share the purchase cost of a vacation accommodation, whether it is a hotel room or condo, cabin or mansion or castle, yacht, cruise ship berth, RV, or houseboat. In return, you get the ability to use that accommodation during a period of time.

Most countries rely on right-to-use systems for their timeshares (a concept we will look more closely at in the next chapter). Purchasing deeded property as a timeshare is nearly exclusive to the United States, where the majority of states make it essential for timeshare sales representatives to be licensed as real estate agents, and for sales and other financial transactions to be overseen by a licensed real estate broker. Though these are not requirements in every state, as a retired financial advisor and real estate investor, I greatly appreciate how the strict regulations and oversight applied to those industries could and should be applied more broadly to the timeshare industry to protect the consumer.

The most traditional timeshare arrangement in the US might look something like this: a year at one vacation house is divided into fifty-two separate week-long units. Fifty of those weeks are sold to fifty separate owners (leaving two weeks each year for annual renovations and maintenance). Each owner would own a deeded interest in 1/50 of the unit, and each share would represent one week of vacation. This system makes vacation home ownership possible for many people who cannot afford a second home.

Purchasing timeshares should never be viewed as a financial investment with the expectation of gaining a profit in either reselling it or renting it to others. Timesharing is an investment in lifestyle, in future holidays, in family time together. About six years ago, my very first timeshare at the Old Guard served as the site for the first annual family reunion away from our individual homes; other subsequent reunions around the country were made possible through my other timeshare ownership arrangements. I have three brothers who fly in from California, Colorado and Texas/Alaska; my self-appointed job is to provide the venue each year. I wouldn't trade that time with them in the beautiful places we have stayed in for any monetary ROI. Visiting our timeshare in North Carolina with a dear friend recently was not only an excellent way to spend safe quality time together—getting her perspective on the key-ready benefits of timeshares in comparison with her own vacation home in Michigan gave me a new level of appreciation for what we have and can share with our loved ones. When viewed that way, I'd say timesharing can be a very good investment indeed!

An ideal vacation at your home away from home, a simple concept—where could the complications, the issues, the problems possibly be?

Chapter 2

MIXING IT UP WORLDWIDE

Building on our initial experience at the Old Guard, the allure of timeshares and other fractional interests attracted my wife and me elsewhere—this time, to a property far from the city that never sleeps. In 2013, the beauty of a small, upscale quiet club in the mountains of western North Carolina came to our attention through a timeshare exchange.

The original marketing material was so enticing—well, here, see for yourself!

Your Home Away from Home—it's a sanctuary in the mountains. The idea of owning a mountain retreat appeals to those who yearn to escape the noise, crowds and confusion of everyday life.

But a retreat should offer more than the opportunity to "get away from it all." It should allow you to reconnect with nature, family, and romance—and help you appreciate life's elemental pleasures, from playing cards beside a roaring fire to marveling at the beauty of a waterfall.

The moment you arrive, you know that you have escaped to a more tranquil world. You check in at the clubhouse, which displays a handsome stone-and-timber façade that blends with the surrounding woodlands. You are welcomed by name in the reception lobby. The concierge arranges dinner reservations at your favorite restaurant and your tee time for the following morning.

Entering your residence, you are greeted by soft music, fresh flowers, a refrigerator stocked with beverages, and a collection of specialty coffees. You instantly feel at home in this three-bedroom haven, which will accommodate your family in rustic elegance.

Just a stroll away from your residence is a two-story clubhouse. Here, you can sit with a cocktail by the massive stone fireplace, read in the library, play darts or billiards, enjoy a sauna in the fitness center, go for a swim, challenge another member to a friendly tennis match, or host a cookout. Surrounding your club are countless recreational opportunities, from golfing to hiking, fly-fishing to fine dining, to antique shopping.

For all its small-town charm, Mountain Lodge offers diverse entertainment. The primary streets are lined with fine restaurants, boutiques, and antique stores. To the southwest is another small town immensely popular among vacationers for its picturesque setting and award-winning dining.

Perched at an elevation of 3,500 feet, the club lies on a highlands plateau. To the south and east, the plateau descends steeply down the Blue Ridge escarpment. This geologic wonder and seasonal precipitation combine to create a beguiling realm of thick forests, clear-running rivers, and abundant waterfalls.

Club owners who fly-fish will discover that the local streams—replete with boulders, plunge pools, narrow shoots and cascades—offer some of the most productive trout waters in the nation. Hikers will find plentiful trails, including one that leads to the highest waterfall east of the Rocky Mountains. State parks, national forests, and a trailhead for the 2,175-mile Appalachian National Scenic Trail are all within a short drive of the club.

Designed for mountain living, the Mountain Lodge residences are an artful blend of civilized comforts and an authentic high-country ambiance.

Encompassing 2,400 square feet, including three bedrooms and three and one-half baths, each handsomely furnished residence offers ample living space. Premium-quality appliances and granite countertops grace the kitchen. Two of the bedrooms are master suites, one featuring a steam shower and the other a walk-in shower and soaking tub. A washer and dryer add extra convenience, and all bath, kitchen, and laundry sundries are provided.

Your home is elegant, yet rustic in all the right places. Wood and stone sheath the exterior, while inside, oak floors and knotty pine ceilings impart cozy warmth. Expansive windows bring nature's beauty inside. Two large decks—one off the great room, the other adjoining a master suite—invite relaxed viewing of the surrounding mountains. In the great room, a large wood-burning fireplace serves as the convivial heart of your home.

Additionally, you enjoy special access to amenities including a health club with spa facility, a tennis center, an executive golf course, two restaurants, a coffee house, a pub, and a golf club. Graced by natural rock formations, hardwood forests, and clear-running streams, the course is unforgettably picturesque. The signature thirteenth hole is a 401-yard par four that aims

down valley from an elevated tee and con-
cludes at a secluded green framed by a cas-
cading waterfall . . .

When we arrived and saw it for ourselves, it was love
at first sight! Unlike New York, there was no sales
presentation at Mountain Lodge—unless you count
my sale to the club director to allow us to join their
ranks. He did, and we've been very happy owners
since.

To me, the prevailing concept was that it was a
country club membership—a different form of timeshare from the Old Guard, and one I believe to be a
far more appealing business model for those in the
luxury vacation home market. Let me elaborate with
more copy from the Mountain Lodge's own original
marketing material:

This is an "equity residence club," offering
the benefits of owning a vacation home—
without the high costs or maintenance
concerns of traditional real estate. So now,
having a family sanctuary in the mountains
is every bit as simple and rewarding as it
should be.

The Privileges of Ownership: As a Mountain Lodge owner, you receive privileges that are simply unavailable with most luxury vacation homes. For starters, our friendly club staff provides concierge service that attends to your every need.

A Better Way to Own: Mountain Lodge represents a new trend in vacation real estate—the equity residence club. Combining elegant accommodations, on-site amenities, and personal service, these clubs grace some of North America's most prestigious destinations.

Like other residence clubs, Mountain Lodge is owned by its members and operated solely for their enjoyment. As an owner, you receive a one-sixth or a one-twelfth undivided deeded interest in a fully furnished, 2,400-square-foot club residence and an interest in the clubhouse facilities and common areas. You can vacation at the club any time you wish, subject only to reservation policies.

One of the most compelling benefits of Mountain Lodge ownership is that you never have to worry about the upkeep, maintenance, and security of your home. Your club handles all of these nuisances. But the best reason to own at Mountain Lodge is to give your family a sanctuary they can visit year after year. Memories from club vacations will become an enduring part of your family lore. And, like any real estate, you can bequeath your club ownership to your children. So they too can own a sanctuary in the mountains.

In retrospect, the significance of this second acquisition has been that, while technically a timeshare, it's really not. It's more of a country club with a board of directors comprised of owners. As owners, we have up to four weeks available each year as "planned vacation;" in addition, we may use the property at any other time, as long as it is open and available.

Types of Timeshares

Mountain Lodge has become more to me than a beautiful and beloved vacation destination; it's opened my eyes to the sheer variety of timeshare arrangements and structures. This runs us right up to one of the most difficult parts of having an intelligent conversation about timeshares in general, much less timeshare industry reform: there are so many different types of timeshares, each with their own (and largely unregulated) terms for the working parts of their systems, and very few no-nonsense guides to the landscape as a whole. Between points, stars, weeks, units, and what have you, it can be hard to tell from resort to resort what, when, and where you are buying interest in.

At the base, every type of timeshare program is selling ownership interest in one of two things: real estate or right of use. When you purchase interest in a **fee simple program**, you are granted an actual, titled deed to a piece of real estate. When you purchase interest in a **right-to-use program**, you are not purchasing any property, but rather the option to use it for a specific period of time. Somewhere in the middle, there are also **leaseholder** options that can be purchased, which grant you the ownership of the property (with both the protections and obligations that entails), but, as with any lease, your ownership expires on a preselected date.

Once you determine whether you are purchasing

real estate or right of use, there are many different ways that timeshare programs structure how and when you can plan your vacation stay.

My first experience with timeshares at the Old Guard is an excellent example of one of the most common timeshare structures: **flex time**. With flex time arrangements, you purchase the number of days out of each year you want to spend in a specific-sized unit. The Old Guard contract year runs from July through June, and I own seven days there annually in one of their penthouse suites; each July, I call the Old Guard and book the days I would like to stay there through the following June. There are significant advantages to flex time arrangements: I can, for example, host a seven-day family reunion there in September one year, and the next year, I can split my time there for a long weekend in June and a few days for Christmas. This flexibility goes both ways, however, and there are also disadvantages, which other timeshare structures work to address.

Popular dates can fill up quickly (who doesn't love New Year's in New York!), and with flex time, I am not guaranteed the dates that I would most prefer; if I was dead set on seeing the ball drop each year in Times Square, I would be better off purchasing interest in a **fixed time** structure, in which I would always be booked into the timeshare for the last week of the calendar year (or any other standing booking I chose at the time of purchase). Fixed time arrangements are often paired with **fixed unit** arrangements, which tackles another potential downside of my Old Guard flex time arrangement: though I may vastly prefer the view from one particular penthouse suite, I am not guaranteed that room when I book, but any one of the twenty or so penthouse suites they have to offer. With a fixed unit arrangement, I would be guaranteed to book exactly the space I wanted.

Fractional ownerships, private residence clubs, and equity residence clubs also offer this type of unit guarantee, albeit usually at a significantly higher price point than most timeshare systems (and usually offering significantly more amenities as well). Mountain Lodge was my first experience with this type of arrangement; as I will argue throughout the book, this system is a model that several other timeshare arrangements can aspire to in terms of reform. Within these systems, ownership of each unit is divided into either fourths, eighths, or twelfths, and each owner is granted an equal number of days each year in which to use the property. There are about twenty-five units at Mountain Lodge, and we own two deeded pieces to our favorite unit, though we don't have to stay there when we visit.

Of course, the loss of flexibility for fixed time/fixed unit arrangements also comes with disadvantages; owning a timeshare ownership in late December would be of no help to me if I wanted to host a family reunion there in September. But what if I knew that I'd be eager some years to trade one week in my penthouse for two weeks in a smaller room? No combination of flex and fixed time/units is structured to address that, so I'd be best suited by another timeshare arrangement: the **points system**. The points system was invented by Vacation Internationale in the early 1970s, and has since become one of the most common means of ownership in traditional timeshares. Though the Old Guard is a timeshare of a singular building, many timeshare companies (including the corporation that controls the Gilded Enigma, which appears later in the book) have many resorts across the country or world. Some of these timeshare behemoths have carefully graded the desirability of each of their units throughout the year and assigned their worth in points. Though you still might be purchasing simple deeded property when you enter into a points system timeshare, the focus is on how much your purchase is worth in points, which is spent within the system like cash. To keep it simple, let's say you have purchased one hundred points at a single resort; you could spend them all for a week in a penthouse with an ocean view during peak season, or you could take three weeks in a smaller room during the off-season. The points system is on the other side of the flexibility spectrum from fixed time to fixed units, with all the advantages and disadvantages that flexibility entails.

Enjoying New Locations

Part of the allure of timeshare ownership that the points system capitalizes on is the ability to exchange time at your "home" property for a completely different property or experience elsewhere, including worldwide exchanges. Even though only one of the timeshare ownerships we have is run on a points system, all of them offer this benefit, either through their own exchanges or through a third party. Our Mountain Lodge property has substantial trading power in the luxury vacation home marketplace. As a result, we have traded a week or longer at our club for a week in even larger, privately owned vacation homes near Yosemite National Park, Mountain Village (Telluride), Colorado, and elsewhere for family reunions.

Because of my affinity for Manhattan, we've only once exchanged time there, many years ago. On the other hand, because of the more abundant time available at the Mountain Lodge, we routinely exchange two weeks there each year through a standalone service operated exclusively for those owning individual second (vacation) homes desiring to use, but not purchase, a third home owned by another. These exchanges are perfect for our annual reunions, because they give us access to a substantial inventory of large, spacious homes throughout the US (and world, as desired) that can easily accommodate all. Even so, we find we still have more than enough time to enjoy our North Carolina mountain property.

Because we prefer this type of exchange, those offered by our other timeshare acquisitions are not particularly attractive to us (something senior timeshare executives simply don't seem to understand). But to many, it's a huge benefit, though also complex and confusing. So, for those unfamiliar, here's a very quick and simplified overview of timeshare exchanges.

With respect to timeshares, the organization facilitating the exchange (normally a subsidiary of the timeshare developer or a third party contracted by the developer) does so for its members. Members are charged an annual fee for the privilege of being among those who may use their services. When used, there is another fee.

Once an exchange is scheduled, the member pays an exchange fee that will vary depending on a number of factors, which may include the relative desirability of properties involved, the seasonal demand of the exchange (e.g., peak season in winter for ski lodges) and the overall value and market demand of the properties involved. Broadly, these exchanges can take many forms. Some are:

Exchanging for weeks, the simplest and most common form of exchange. Here you exchange time, usually a week, at your home property for time at another, presumed to be of equal value. Of course, there are endless variations. As an example, if your home property is of greater value than the one you seek, you could receive a trading "credit" and use it for, perhaps, a second vacation. And if your home property is of lesser value, you could combine multiple deposits and/

or credits (for a fee) and trade-up for a nicer vacation experience.

Exchanging for points, which provides greater flexibility on where and when to travel, together with choosing the size and quality of accommodations. Points typically accrue with payment of annual maintenance fees paid to the timeshare and/or through membership programs.

In 1974, a mere year after the word "timeshare" was first used to describe this growing vacationing system, one couple, Jon and Christel DeHaan, invented the first exchange company—Resort Condominiums International (RCI), which is still one of the major players in the timeshare exchange market today. Just as the invention of fractional ownership saved the sales of resort condominiums during a period of economic stagnation, the DeHaans saw how they could increase the value of timeshares exponentially— without developing a single one. If timeshare owners were not only buying a vacation, but entry into a whole system of vacation possibilities, the value of their purchase would be much higher.

Visionaries like the DeHaans not only brought a

new way of vacationing to the world but, over time, literally revolutionized the motel and hotel industries and the way millions of travelers vacation . . . but should they?

Chapter 3

NEW ACQUISITIONS AND QUESTIONS

In 2016, I was staying at the Old Guard while helping a friend find a suitable upscale Midtown hotel for a future visit. I came upon the perfect one . . . or so I thought. Upon inquiring about amenities, rates, etc., I was surprised at the relatively small size of the lobby area.

Was it a hotel? No.

Midtown Modernity (MM) was a timeshare offered by a major, international hotel brand. The ad that had attracted me was an offer to use one of the units as a short-term hotel suite during the offseason.

Compared with the Old Guard, it was much newer

and filled with additional perks. Of special attraction was the long penthouse balcony; within the suite, floor-to-ceiling glass provided an excellent panorama of the city with unobstructed views. The key was its openness, along with the usual luxurious things: fine linens, flat-screen TVs, spacious bathrooms, etc. It was still within easy walking distance of Carnegie Hall, Central Park, Fifth Avenue shopping, Rockefeller Center, Broadway, Radio City Music Hall, Jazz at Lincoln Center, and everything else the Big Apple has to offer. Paired with its famed "Billionaires Row" location, this was irresistible.

Did my wife and I need two Midtown Manhattan timeshares? Probably not, but MM was an attractive complement to the Old Guard. Whereas the first was "old luxury" with its greater square footage, the second was "new luxury," with its open feel and all the latest gadgets.

Although the costs and annual maintenance fees were substantially higher than those at the Old Guard, we found it comparable to a private residence club. (Though it billed itself as a "club," it was actually a standard fee-simple timeshare.) I refocused on our financial situation objectively, as if we were one of my clients. I had not yet retired as a licensed financial advisor, so my business was helping others on such issues, including retirement income and estate distribution. Key to that was a form of cash flow modeling that I found particularly useful (and continue to use). Fortunately, the results confirmed the new acquisition with its ongoing costs to be within our means, and on April 13, 2016, my wife and I purchased an ownership interest equal to about a week each calendar year in a suite at MM for the asking price.

But my modeling had sparked a new interest and focus that remains today: the entire timeshare business and its business model. Despite my attempts to have all my concerns addressed prior to purchase, several disconcerting elements had popped up later. After six months of MM ownership, on October 21, 2016, I started reflecting on the first statement of expenses I'd received and realized I still had more questions than answers. As I resolved to learn more about this "beast" and how it operates, I would soon discover I was treading on sacred ground! I became both a fan and critic of timeshares—a cognitive dissonance that the timeshare executives would not understand, beginning from the very first correspondence I sent on that day. Personally, I thought my questions and requests in that initial email, which eventually landed on the desk of Ron as part of the MM sales management, were quite reasonable:

> **Questions/Request**: Just prior to purchase, I asked the salesperson (and others): "How did you come up with the price?" I never got a good answer, so I'll ask again here. **Apart from determining desired net profit and what the market will bear, what additional factors, if any, went into arriving at this price?** I'm not complaining; I just want to be an informed consumer. My purpose is to gain better insight into your business model. Candor would be appreciated.
>
> Additionally, for context and perspective, it would be useful to know two things: (1) the average asking price for selected units over time, together with the average amount actually paid by purchasers (if different); and (2) assuming it is non-recoverable, the average commission paid, as a percentage of sales price, for selected units.

Feedback/Observation: As a financial advisor, I have cautioned others that time-shares, in general, are a waste of money because the heavy up-front "load" and ongoing maintenance fees tend to outweigh benefits. Yet, here I am. This imbalance was recently underscored when I learned of the lowball Midtown Modernity buy-back offer. Now, to be clear, I have neither intention nor desire to sell. But I feel that as part of my fiduciary duty, I must know more about what goes on behind the scenes. Thus, your cooperation and candor would be appreciated.

That said, it's apparent the resale program is another Midtown Modernity profit center. I have no problem with that, but it begs the question why owners are presented *misinformation* about how to use it. Here's what I mean.

When resale questions arise, Midtown Modernity call center employees are taught to direct owners to the "Resale Department." Makes sense, but here's my experience. To learn more, I left a voice mail inquiry on 7/29/2016. Having heard nothing by late

September, I complained to the call center that the department seems, at best, to be inattentive, or at worst, a sham and concluded Midtown Modernity had no real interest in helping members with resales. Interestingly, however, my complaint resulted in a call back from the department in early October. After trading several voicemails, our conversation resulted in two areas of further concern: (1) the aforementioned low-ball number (I was told my buy-back offer would be about 25 percent sales price); and (2) the Resale Department is not the correct place to call. Instead, I'm told, it's the "Member Support Department," and members call there only when they've found a prospective buyer. As I understand it, a member should only call the Resale Department as a last resort. I think it important to train call center employees accordingly and incorporate a discussion of the relative illiquidity of these fractional interests during the sales process because of the [blank].

In view of the above and as a final observation on my situation, if the delta between amounts paid and resale value (sales price minus 75 percent) is correct, this buyer has quite a bit of imputed equity, suggesting a great deal of additional value will be delivered by Midtown Modernity over the course of ownership. And with payment of annual maintenance fees, it further suggests any gratuities, et cetera, paid for its use going forward will have been <u>prepaid</u> well in advance. [Recipient was asked to complete my statement by filling in the blank.]

Five days later, I received a response—or, rather, I received an email—in return. Ron thanked me for my questions and observations before advising me that most of the requested data was proprietary—not for public disclosure. He also imagined that my assumption about the rationale for prices was correct and asserted there was no difference in asking price and selling price—they did not negotiate prices (a point I would later refute by digging deep into the bowels of the disclosure documents). He advised me that salesperson compensation was paid by seller, not buyer.

According to Ron, the Resale Department was a relatively small office because the expectation was that most new owners are buying for a lifetime and beyond (for heirs). The Resale Department was created only as it was not always possible for one to keep their ownership forever, and many such owners have neither the time nor knowledge to list their ownership interest themselves, transfer title, et cetera. He volunteered to speak to management and trainers about sales staff and call center Resale Department training, but offered no additional information or promised action.

I was disappointed to find that nothing further was forthcoming, and dashed off a quick acknowledgement later that day:

> In the midst of our current travels, your timely response was most welcome. Thank you for it.
>
> Unfortunately, while it no doubt sailed through compliance, and perhaps because of it, you must have known that it would be received for what it is, largely useless. Sorry you got stuck with this. At least you answered the mail.
>
> It seems the inner workings of the process are as much a mystery to you as MM's parent

company wishes to make it for me. Proprietary information is another way of saying it's none of your business. I disagree and am disappointed. I'll continue elsewhere.

WHC

Forging Ahead

Although I had every intention of following up further, life got in the way, and soon enough, I was on to other things—including another timeshare purchase. The international corporation from which we had purchased our MM timeshare had an even more modern and luxurious offering under construction a few blocks away. (Obviously, the timeshare business in NYC is good!) While we couldn't justify yet another Midtown timeshare, we decided to "trade in" our MM shares (plus cash) for two units there, making them our fourth and last. When the project was completed some eighteen months later, we upgraded from Midtown Modernity to the Gilded Enigma (GE).

We first used our newest property for a family reunion in September 2018 and fell in love anew.

In fact, we've become so delighted with it that I (or we) drive up about once a month for two or three nights for both business and pleasure. We know and enjoy the members of the staff. Together with many others, they make the property what we've come to see as our "home away from home." The upgrades are truly impressive, and the much higher top-floor penthouse suites command an amazing panoramic view of Midtown and Central Park to the north.

Because of this, we now use the GE for most of our New York visits, with the Old Guard and its greater space as a welcome diversion.

While we enjoyed MM and hosted one of our family reunions there, my concerns about their business operations were never resolved. Consequently, when the first annual maintenance fee statement for the GE arrived, I examined it and its attachments thoroughly. I am not unskilled in reading financial documents— as a retired and formerly licensed financial advisor, I likely have considerably more experience than the average individual—but I was left with more questions than answers as I reviewed the statement. Since much of it defied logic, I responded in writing with a series of questions and observations, beginning a series of mostly one-way communication that ultimately led to my meeting with a senior executive of the parent company overseeing both MM and GE (we'll call him Adam)—and to this book.

On January 15, 2019, I sent my questions in an email to Lucy, the GE club director:

> As I seek to better understand the business and legal underpinnings of the HOA, I need answers to certain questions about how the operation conducts its business. The purpose is to help me become a more informed advocate and, as a result, better able to make meaningful decisions and constructive input about our "home away from home."

1. Please help me understand the meaning of these terms used in materials sent:

    a. Condominium Declaration: What is it? Who creates it and under what authority?

    b. Timeshare Declaration: What is it? Who creates it and under what authority?

c. Declaration and Association By-Laws: Who creates these and under what authority?

d. Declaration of Covenants, Conditions and Restrictions and Ownership: What are these and how may owners have a copy?

e. Declarant: Exactly who or what is it?

f. Subsidy Agreement: What is it? Why does it matter? May owners get a copy?

g. Sponsor: Who or what is it? How does it fit in with other players?

h. The Association: What is it? Am I to assume it's the HOA?

2. Please address these additional, basic questions:

a. What is the purpose of "Club Dues"? Why are they broken out as a separate fee? Wouldn't it be better to simply provide whatever goods and services they convey as a matter of normal business, instead of charging separately?

b. Most developers/HOA creators "adopt" certain boilerplate documents and assume owners will accept them as written. Where are the governing documents for the HOA, and how may owners (through HOA) amend them, if deemed appropriate and/or necessary?

c. Must owners accept the judgment of "Declarant" (whoever that is) if they have reason to disagree?

d. How are initial maintenance fees determined?

e. Is it incomprehensible that maintenance fees may actually go down?

f. To whom are we paying the management fee?

g. When it comes to resources, what is the chain of authority governing HOA administrative (labor) and operational expenses? What comprises the "Condominium Common Expense Allocation"?

h. Why do the annual budget footnotes say the HOA has "no sources of income"?

i. What is "The Management Agreement" between our HOA and the Gilded Enigma Manager? Who sets the fees shown therein? May owners (the HOA) get a copy?

j. What is a "Brand Services Fee"?

k. Who is "The Manager"?

l. Who approves the "Other Expenses"?

m. Do we really have no control over the enormous sums spent for housekeeping?

n. What is "The Condominium" and who/what pays it for operational supplies and service, to include housekeeping, et cetera?

o. How irreversibly are we entangled with existing labor agreements? Why are we so entangled? Can we get out of them? If so, what does it take? What are the consequences? Are owners obliged because others have agreed to them? Are such disclosures made to owners at time of sale in writing? If so, are they reasonably understandable? What rights vis-à-vis the HOA do owners have? From materials provided, I see that certain union contract(s) expire shortly. What options do owners have? Who is really "the boss" when it comes to running the Gilded Enigma Suites Owners Association, Inc.?

p. Who or what determines the sales price of any particular ownership interest at any particular time? Once the "Grantee" pays it, how does your company use the proceeds—and for what purpose? May I assume sales commissions are a major part? If so, and if such sales efforts are key to a purchase, can owners expect similar efforts (for sums already paid) to be made on their behalf (say, after a period of time) to be used for a resale? If ownership interest is a valued entity, assuming property is well-maintained, why are resales always assumed to be of less value? Is it incomprehensible that sales (resale) prices may ever go up?

3. Here are some observations:

   a. The HOA gives me the initial impression of being run "on the cheap." I say that because it seems to treat owners as nothing special . . . e.g., using non-postage paid return envelopes to collect dues checks (minor but telling), discouraging use of credit cards (seems insane after the sales department insists on their use). As a thought, instead of discouraging credit cards, HOA should give owners a discount for paying by check—especially when it apparently charges owners for using them (see budget).

   b. In your welcoming letter introducing owners to their annual maintenance fee statements, you provide a phone number and say, "If you have any questions regarding your annual statement, please call."

That sounds good, but, unfortunately, the person(s) on the other end of that line have no clue. They haven't been trained to respond to likely owner questions about materials sent them.

c.   Finally, I appreciate the phrase used at the bottom of your forwarding letter! I believe it encapsulates the desired result of any effort it might take to have an informed, satisfied, engaged, and committed ownership:

"... we look forward to welcoming you back to the familiar comfort of your home away from home."

Dean, an executive at the Management Firm associated with both GE and MM (referred to hereafter as MF), called me in response on February 1, 2019; our conversation was cordial, but again, not terribly satisfying. Perhaps what I heard is best summed up with the phrase, "It is what it is . . ."

Essentially, we agreed that most of my questions could be answered by information that I should have already had. But did I? He mentioned a USB drive that I should have received from the sales department, but volunteered to mail one to me. That was good, because while I got a nice leather-encased USB from Sales, it had no HOA info on it.

He told me what "club dues" were, but didn't say why they were broken out as a separate fee, and told me maintenance fees were simple math based on costs divided by number and type of ownership contracts. I was instructed to always think of maintenance fees going up, never down, and that the rate increase would be about 5 percent per year.

The "management fee" (some of the HOA fee) was paid to Dean and others to "manage" our affairs. I was still left puzzled, unsure it was worth that much to us . . . why?

The "brand fee" was for our ability to use the Parent Company's (PC) name. But did we want or need it? Were we required to do so? It seemed too high and went up every year as well. Why must it be this much? How many profit centers must PC and the GE have?

I received the promised documents, which I had, indeed, never seen before. In retrospect, I would have liked the opportunity to fully review them prior to purchase, and I believe all prospective owners should be given this opportunity. I had hoped to include a redacted version in this book, so that others could read through just an example, but legal counsel advised against it. Thus, you will have to rely on the questions and concerns I had after reviewing my documents to inform your own review, though I have included a glossary of simplified definitions in Appendix 10.

After fully reviewing the documents, on February 28, 2019, I sent a substantive letter expressing additional areas of concern with questions and observations and asked for input prior to the HOA Board meeting. It read, in part:

> I'm concerned with what I see as an inherent conflict of interest for the Gilded Enigma's PC as it attempts to serve both its stockholders and customers (owners) like us. While corporate commentary suggests otherwise, I'm not so sure.
>
> Moreover, my opinions expressed in certain "observations" below go beyond documents and may be construed as consumer complaints. If so, others within the GE PC may wish to comment for the record.

While knowing it's necessary, I don't like the overuse of "boilerplate" that comprises most business communication, including language within GE documents. Thus, I'd appreciate responses in writing that are thoughtful and frank. So, let's be real. Because the term "timeshare" is a pejorative in many circles, I want to help remove the stigma. Stated simply, I'd like to make the enterprise of which I consider myself a part better.

Here are my initial questions and observations. About half relate to subjects addressed in my response to the HOA Statement package, while the rest are those about the GE Suites Management Agreement (MA). So here they are:

1. Since I'm planning to attend the 2019 Annual Meeting, can you tell me what time of day it's likely to be scheduled?

2. May I assume that initial Association (HOA) Board Members are GE employees? Are they expected to attend the annual meeting?

3. Regarding a "brand services fee," I suppose it is what it is, but I'm not clear why such exists. As stated in the MA, it covers mandatory programs and services that are deemed beneficial to the Project's operations. I get it, but at a property like Gilded Enigma where owners pay a premium to get in, it seems reasonable to assume such services are a given—without need to pay an additional fee. Other than being in the documents, what is the justification? Is such provision unique to the Gilded Enigma?

4. Regarding the Subsidy Agreement, it seems to be what the name implies, a sponsor subsidy paid to HOA during a project's early years. Is that it or is there a potential downside to owners if its termination is ill-timed? If so, can you please elaborate?

5. The documents refer to the most prevalent common area as the "Owner's Lounge," yet a plaque mounted at the GE calls it "Member's Lounge." Is there a reason for this? Aside from cost and owner preference, is there any reason why it couldn't be changed to read "Owner's Lounge"?

6. How irreversibly are we entangled with existing labor agreements? Can we get out of them? If so, what does it take and who would undertake the task? What are the consequences? Disclosure of labor agreements are not made to prospective owners at time of sale, but they should be. From materials provided, I see that certain union contract(s) expire shortly. What options do Management Firm (MF)/HOA have with respect terminating or modifying?

7. Regarding my original question about source of sales prices, I see the answer in the documents. My question now is this: are listed sales prices somewhat analogous to MSRP of a new auto? Of course, this would have been nice to have at time of sale, or beforehand . . .

    Observation 7: If MSRP is a reasonable analogy, there's a dramatic drop in value once driven off the lot! That aside, while the GE sales process is no doubt robust and drives the business model, it's notably weak, at least by financial service standards, in one important area with which I became familiar in my most recent career, compliance. For example, there's no attempt at any kind of financial underwriting or consumer risk tolerance, despite the first page of Timeshare Offering screaming of RISK (but what kind of risk?). Yet, if my experience is like others, customers do not see any documents timely. And because documents are not available for review before or during the sale, consumers have no idea until afterward that the quoted "price," like MSRP, is entirely negotiable. Nor do they have any idea of the "Hotel California" effect, to say nothing of illiquidity. If the Timeshare Act and related regulations don't require timely disclosure, it should. From my perspective, it's malpractice. So, it's unlikely consumers have reviewed (or been given) documents before the sale, yet the closing process requires them to acknowledge in a "Statement of Understanding" that project documents override anything they may have heard during the sales process. Obviously, the main purpose is to absolve the GE PC of liability, not facilitate an informed buying decision. Finally, I suspect many (if not most) who buy neither understand nor fully comprehend the significance of their decision. For those who may desire it, has the GE PC considered providing them with an "advocate" during the sales process? Just a thought: as an owner who's been through it a few times, I may be able to help.

8. Once more, let's consider the world of automobile leases. If one were to imagine a timeshare sales price to be like a "cap cost reduction" provision in leases (after all, I expect most GE profit comes after the sale), why is there no reduction in lease payments (annual maintenance)? It then begs the question originally asked: where, in general, does the GE PC use the sales proceeds—and for what purpose? While I could speculate on this, I'd rather not. If ownership interest is a valued entity, assuming property is well maintained, why are resales always assumed to be of far less (approaching zero) value? Is it incomprehensible that sales prices (for resale) may ever hold value?

Observation 8: Of course, all this stirs my interest in the timeshare industry business model, including the GE's. This is not to say it's bad—just unduly secretive. I'm perfectly willing to sign whatever nondisclosure the GE or others may require. The lack of transparency, cloaked as "proprietary," is troublesome. I'd like to be considered a team member, not an "outsider" whose motives are unknown. Reasonable sunlight and openness are good things, especially if they can promote confidence in the industry. I believe informed owners can be among the GE's most valued assets—strong advocates who, in turn, could become centers of influence. Only then can they state with confidence to others that the business operation is fair and makes sense. I'm committed to the GE project and would like to help develop an army of raving fans. Is the GE willing to help?

9. Why does the HOA encourage owners to pay maintenance fees by check? How many actually pay that way? In so doing, the HOA gives one the initial impression of being run "on the cheap" on small things.

Observation 9: Discouraging use of credit cards seems insane after the sales department insists on their use as part of the closing process. Instead of discouraging credit cards, Management Firm/HOA should consider giving owners a discount for paying by check, especially when HOA budget includes a substantial allowance for credit card fees.

10. Why aren't appropriately trained employees available to answer predicable questions about the annual statement package?

Observation 10: In your welcoming letter introducing owners to their annual maintenance fee statements, you provide a phone number with a suggestion that says: "If you have any questions regarding your annual statement, please call." That sounds good but, unfortunately, the person(s) on the other end of the line have no clue. It's not their fault. They just haven't been trained to respond to likely owner questions.

11. Regarding management authority in the Management Agreement (MA), I see that MA has authority to supervise and direct all phases of advertising, sales, reservations, and business promotion for the Project. This seems an odd distraction for a management firm. Is it? Will you please elaborate to help me better understand any benefits that might accrue to owners.

12. Related to delegation and as we discussed by phone, please elaborate on the awkward and costly situation created in the past by the Board wherein they hired and paid an outside contractor (ostensibly to save money) only to be billed a greater amount afterward by the Condominium as a "penalty" for not using them?

13. As stated in the MA, and as confirmed in the footnote to the HOA 2019 Annual Budget, the MA has an initial term of five years with an expiration in 2020. Yet, I seem to recall seeing a new "restart" date somewhere in the documents. Was the footnote in error? If so, will you please confirm the date and term of the current agreement?

14. I see the Management Firm (MF) has the right to "make mandatory Services optional, or to make optional Services mandatory . . ." Does this include maid service under a union contract? Apparently so, as footnotes attached to the 2019 annual statement package include an option to reduce housekeeping cleans to two per week. If owners desire, what does it take to make this happen?

15. The subject of MF's marketing various products, including, without limitation, vacation ownership interests or other real property interests, comes up again. Is this a collateral duty or a significant part the GE PC's sales and marketing pursuits? Apparently, it's the latter. As stated, MF shall be the exclusive agent for on-site and off-site rental and resales services. Are you self-supervised?

16. Please help me understand this potential special assessment that may be levied in the manner prescribed in the Bylaws, including, but not limited to, the collection of an annual fee for lobbying and legislative efforts beneficial to the HOA. Can you provide me with some insight into what kind of lobbying and legislative efforts such an assessment might cover?

17. Regarding bank accounts, can you provide some insight regarding types of account(s) now in use for Reserve Funds? What is the total balance now in reserve?

18. Within those managed properties having over two hundred fifty members, how many (if any) have undertaken self-management? Of those, does MF continue to provide reservation system and exchange services for them?

19. Regarding management fee, there is a specific percentage shown. Can you please clarify and/or correct my quick calculation from the 2019 budget? It shows Management Fees which, divided by total expected Association Fees, results in a larger percentage. Is the difference due to the addition of Financial Services and Brand Fees to the Management Fee, making it plural (fees)?

20. Related to above, Financial Services and Brand Services Fees are not shown on the 2019 Budget. May I assume they're embedded within the management fees?

21. The marketing function comes up again, wherein MF may, from time to time, at its sole cost and expense . . . market and sell such products and services as it desires . . . including, without limitation, vacation ownership interests or other property interests in the project. It strikes me this distracts MF from focusing on its primary function, that of management. If so, how does this make sense to our members? If not, apart from being "baked" into the agreement, why must we allow this?

22. It says the HOA delegates to MF the right to enforce all rules and regulations. How does MF do this from afar? And can it do so effectively?

It felt like a start, and I looked forward to getting some answers. However, in retrospect (and in my opinion), this is where the Gilded Enigma stonewalling truly began. By March 12, I was more concerned with finding out if my email had even been received! In the face of stony silence, I sent another email to Lucy, the GE club director, to make sure:

"Statement of Understanding"

Whereas W.H. Campbell, owner of two ownership interests in the Gilded Enigma, has sent an email communication attaching a letter to Dean, an MF executive, on the morning of February 28, 2019, asking certain questions and conveying certain observations; and whereas Dean has neither acknowledged receipt nor responded to a voicemail asking for same; and whereas part of Mr. Campbell's concern, as expressed in the letter, was an apparent "secrecy" with which the Gilded Enigma conducts its business; and finally, whereas the lack of acknowledgment seems to confirm the assertion, this statement of agreement from his representative is sought.

Statement of Agreement:

As noted above and understanding Mr. Campbell's concern that Dean has not received his communication, I hereby agree to send the original to him via approved and secure Gilded Enigma means as I have in the past. Doing so and following up to ensure

receipt by him is at Mr. Campbell's request.
Lucy
Club Director

Or

Statement of Agreement:

As noted above and understanding Mr. Campbell's concern that Dean has not received his communication, I hereby confirm that I personally know of his having already received it on or about _____.
Thus, there is no need to send anything further to him at this time.

Lucy
Club Director

That, at least, got a response—later that day, Lucy verbally confirmed Dean had received my email, but also informed me that she was not permitted to sign anything. Hmm . . .

On March 22, 2019, I finally heard from Dean. I missed the call, but he followed up via email. He advised me that he had tried to call to discuss my February 28 letter and asked me to call back at my convenience. He also advised me when, exactly, the GE Board meeting would be held, but the "where" would only be available to me upon returning his call.

I quickly responded:

Hi Dean,

Sorry to have missed your call. But it's just as well.

As you should know, I don't wish to discuss the letter by phone.

Instead, as mentioned in my letter, I'd appreciate a response(s) in writing that is thoughtful and frank. If you can't meet the desired timeframe, I understand and can wait. But it's important. I like the Gilded Enigma and am serious about doing what I can to help make it the best it can be.

I look forward to seeing you at the Board Meeting.

WHC

I had my questions, and I had a venue with a captive audience of people with the information I needed— surely, I'd find my answers there . . .

Chapter 4
THE "BODY SNATCHERS"

Before we delve any further into the labyrinth of the timeshare industry, I should clear up a few points. "Why," you might be asking, "do you believe that these industry officials have any incentive to answer your questions?"

Well, although it may not be apparent by looking at a timeshare balance sheet, their most important asset, the one driving future cash flow and profits, is their membership. And these timeshare officials now so eager to avoid me are usually quite eager—insistent, in fact—on engaging.

While we are sometimes referred to as owners or members, I believe it more accurate to call us tenants. As a landlord, I see us more as tenants than real estate owners or country club members. But to include all, I'll refer to us here as owners/members/tenants (OMTs).

Recognizing their best prospects are OMTs, the timeshare industry takes care to encourage and cultivate our return visits to these home resorts. After all, the industry knows that those who've bought once, and presumably enjoyed the experience, are their best candidates to buy again in the form of an upgrade.

I like to separate the industry into two broad parts with this analogy:

Consider this . . . you're enjoying an elegant dinner with some of your best friends where everything is provided for you and every part is as near perfect as you can imagine.

You might start with some delightful libations in a happy hour setting, followed by appetizers so good you just can't refuse, and then on to a fresh salad followed by a main course, perhaps a shared presentation of seafood and filet mignon. You subtly realize the food and drink are exquisite and the service so impeccable you don't even notice the wait staff. But then, your host surprises all with a sublime chocolate mousse dessert. How good does it get? That's the first part, the **banquet**.

And the like, in terms of service and luxury, is routinely delivered by staffs at high-end timeshares, better called resorts. It's there for the taking, plus much more, whenever you decide to visit. And best of all, it is really like being at home and at the destination of your choice at once.

For those enjoying such treatment in the heart of New York City, it's like living in the middle of everything on a tiny fraction of the cost. Best of all, once you're a member, all you have to do is show up and enjoy, while avoiding the enormous property taxes that would otherwise accrue while owning such properties outright. You get all that for paying a relatively modest annual fee.

What I've described (perhaps without the menu) is the **banquet**. It's your reward and the lifestyle choice you made when purchasing a timeshare. The timeshare officials on the banquet side, like Lucy, are pictures of charm, graciousness, and bounty. That's not to say they'll answer any question (as I learned firsthand)—but they are well-equipped to provide the distractions that make a hard-hitting query seem like a rude quibble rather than an urgent matter.

The other, second part of the timeshare industry is the **kitchen—the "sausage factory"** behind it all. It's the rather reclusive nuts and bolts part of the operation where members/owners are not invited because it's considered proprietary. Pushing past the banquet attendants with my inconvenient questions, I have interacted with the kitchen far more than most OMTs. But, like it or not, there is one timeshare position between the banquet and the kitchen that all OMTs can expect to interact with. It begins with an invitation for an "update," which is not so much an update as it is a new opportunity to upgrade our memberships—with, of course, some type of carrot to induce attendance.

Enter the "Body Snatchers."

That's the term widely used by observers to label those whose primary or secondary job is to get others, especially pre-qualified OMTs, to attend sales presentations packaged as updates.

The fact that OMTs are considered to be both pre-qualified and the best prospects is underscored by the degree to which we are courted, both upon arrival and well before, by some aggressive recruiters (aka body snatchers).

At the Old Guard, this invitation usually comes as a phone call to our suite an hour or so after we've checked in and settled, just to confirm that all's good with the experience so far, to learn more of our plans for the stay ahead and, of greatest importance, to be sure we're able to squeeze in enough time for an update as soon into our stay as possible. Doing so, of course, would result in a carrot; I have been offered Broadway tickets and vouchers to collaborating upscale restaurants.

If we agreed, a follow-up system takes over to ensure attendance. The congeniality of the invitation, its follow-up, and the early stages of the presentation are usually followed by what some would characterize as a hard sell experience. However, we generally found it easy enough to disengage. Altogether, the experience there was only mildly discomfiting.

With respect to our private residence club, the Mountain Lodge (ML), the operation is so understated that anything resembling body snatcher activity is nowhere to be found. In fact, if we wanted to upgrade in one way or another, it would catch them as a surprise.

But this is certainly not the case with Midtown Modernity (MM), and even less so with the Gilded Enigma (GE). Part of my purpose here is to influence these and other high-end timeshares to operate more like ML. It only makes sense, since they have entry prices and maintenance fees that exceed those of ML.

So who are these body snatchers? That's an interesting question. Surely, there's no one with such a job description. Some work in the area of guest services or sales/marketing, but I'm convinced many are general administrative types with base salaries who, as an incentive, are also compensated with a commission (or something similar) on any new business that results from their referrals. Perhaps they're trying their wings at sales to see if it fits.

At any rate, MM and GE have exceeded others in perfecting the art of snatching bodies—or, at least, attempting to do so. It starts with a welcoming email hailing the excitement of our pending arrival, counting the days, etc. And it continues with another email and then voice mail(s) reminding us what's new in the city, what's new with this and other projects under development, etc., and the eager anticipation of our arrival. The communiques are generally friendly in nature and without much of an overly "sales-y" pitch. But, to be sure, it's all about business.

These messages are couched in the assumption that both my spouse and I (as cotrustees) will be traveling. Of course, this is because they want all decision-makers (OMTs) present in order to eliminate an obvious objection. Since my spouse strongly dislikes these "updates," she would save her travel for destinations without them. Thus, it would be my common refrain, upon being so approached, to say, "No, thanks." The declination was both effective and final, as it's known to be an industry standard.

However, there was an exception: one particular scheduled December trip to enjoy New York City enticed my spouse to join me. I wanted to experience one of these "updates" in person, so I convinced her to suffer through a presentation where I could learn more, refuse any offer, and then see if we were still offered the carrot—an attractive voucher we could take to one of our favorite Midtown restaurants. My usual body snatcher was both flabbergasted and delighted, and all was set up for us to attend.

The time came, and we checked in at the welcome desk and assumed our seat in the waiting area, complete with expansive views of the Midtown skyline, light music, and an inviting continental breakfast buffet. We waited for what seemed like too long before a young man, obviously full of himself (we'll call him Sparky), appeared to greet us. We went to his work area and had some initial introductory chit-chat.

Of course, Sparky had our profile, such as it was, before him, and he seemed to sense a wonderful upgrade in our future. He saw our current ownership arrangement as good but not optimal; by rearranging our ownership and swapping one aspect of it for another of similar value, he said we'd be awarded more points (thus, even more time to enjoy NYC) with roughly the same annual maintenance fee. It seemed agreeable enough, but when I asked about any associated fees to facilitate the swap, he confirmed that everything they do, even a "swap," involves administrative costs; this was no exception. That made sense, but I wanted to hear more.

Opining the cost (that I would politely decline) might be something on the order of an annual maintenance fee, Sparky's expression turned to disappointment and then disdain—hurt that I'd think his professional insight to be of so little value. So, I pressed him to check the cost within his proprietary software, but he said that would be unnecessary. Once he revealed the number (it was several times the maintenance fee), I told him it was way out of line with reality. I was curious how in the world they'd come up with such a lofty price tag in the first place. But he ignored that train of thought.

Instead, confident that we still desired and could easily afford the offer, Sparky then proceeded to walk out of the room to allow us to talk privately, as if there was some disagreement between us. In fact, before leaving, he informed us that he *knew* we had the money. How did he know this since he had no real financial information about us? The audacity!

It was getting rather amusing for me, if not my spouse. I wanted to see what Sparky brought out of his hat next.

Upon his return, I assured him that, while we had no interest before he left, we had even less now. But still, I wanted to see his next move. And it was to summon his sales manager to confirm the cost he'd stated for the swap (upgrade, in his mind) was valid and in line with the sales and administrative services provided. It was, we were told.

Still, I told Sparky this made absolutely no sense, whereupon he declared something I soon forgot, but my spouse found particularly offensive and unforgettable: "You don't know what you don't know." Hmm...

For me, the experience helped confirm an early

interest in telling the entire timeshare story. For my spouse, it gave her even more reason to never attend any such "update" again. So much for the timeshare image!

(Yes, for what it's worth, we did collect our carrot—and dinner was delicious.)

As with all companies and the industries within which they operate, the timeshare industry is threatened by many potential external and internal risks, as outlined in company annual reports. However, the timeshare industry seems disproportionately and uniquely at risk by one risk: the faith and confidence of OMTs and the consuming public at large in the integrity of the industry and in its products.

You see, while the timeshare industry makes most of its money from existing OMTs after the first sale through their continued membership, it is heavily reliant on having a healthy stream of new prospects as a predictor of the future—including OMTs who may upgrade. But I believe the industry's business model is based on a faulty premise, in part because they are selling to the wrong economic demographic. In short, I believe their profits are most at risk because they are built on a foundation that's at risk.

The fact that about two-thirds of eventual OMTs

find it necessary to secure a loan (with egregious rates) from their timeshare company in order to facilitate a purchase is very telling and is a testament to three things: (1) it's how the sales department works, with a loan typically the default method of payment in the contract; (2) it's how beautiful future cash flows, including those that can be monetized on a balance sheet, appear on timeshare financials; and, sadly, (3) how poorly prospective OMTs are vetted. As a retired financial advisor, I don't see these loan-saddled OMTs as suitable candidates—and that's the majority of purchasers.

Now, when defaults occur (and they do), the timeshare company can buy back the defaulting ownership interest and eventually sell it again at a profit. But this is neither a practical nor sustainable formula, especially if default rates rise. It's so much better to build a business on a solid foundation, with suitable OMTs (or at least satisfied ones) as customers.

But as it now stands, the industry seems to have assigned a high degree of confidence in the business philosophy once espoused by P. T. Barnum in operating his famed American Museum in Lower Manhattan: "There's a sucker born every minute."

Indeed, timeshares are good—but continue reading

this book before buying one! Understand that the majority of buyers are not (at least in the eyes of this observer) suitable, and that the industry can count on fewer "suckers" going forward as a result of this book and other rays of light into their dark spaces. If the body snatchers are fleeing from interacting with this suitable OMT and his questions, something has gone very wrong.

Chapter 5

A LOOK AT THE TIMESHARE BUSINESS MODEL FROM THE REAL ESTATE INVESTOR'S PERSPECTIVE

As a real estate investor myself, I am very interested (and envious!) of the timeshare business model. Think about it—throughout your life, you've heard that investing in real estate is a good way to build wealth and financial freedom, particularly for those acquiring multiple income-producing properties. While it seemed like a good idea at first, the initial costs and ongoing mortgage payments, together with maintenance, property taxes and the rest, dissuaded you from action. You're certainly not alone.

But what if none of these problems were present? Would that have spurred you to action?

Seriously, think about that for a moment. You would have rental income with no ongoing costs like mortgage payments, property taxes or maintenance. Sounds better, right? The only major concern would be keeping leases in place.

But wait—what if even that problem could be eliminated? Yes, what if you were able to find good tenants who were willing to sign leases that *never expire*? How might that affect your peace of mind and rate of return? Under those circumstances, would there be any reason *not* to move forward?

Well, if you're still balking, you might be interested in knowing that it gets even better.

A traditional real estate investment strategy usually involves owning rental properties that generate rising net income with better cost containment over time. Often, the early years are challenging, but over time, cash flows become more predictable and a source of increased financial security for the owner.

Now, instead of owning property to rent, what if you owned property to sell? Stay with me now . . . how about instead of selling the physical property, you sell the right to *use* the property to others as a deeded interest? How might that work?

Let's say a man nearing retirement (we'll call him Jim) is concerned about his financial readiness and seeks professional advice.

> **JIM:** I've saved money for my retirement—but I know it's not enough. In order to make me whole, I want an additional pension (or something like it) with a cost of living provision to give me an additional six-figure income stream per year. Do you have any ideas?

> **ADVISOR:** What do I look like, some kind of miracle worker?? Well, actually, I might. Do you care if it's sort of related to rental income?

> **JIM:** That's fine, but I don't have any rental properties or extra money to get any.

> **ADVISOR:** Don't worry. All you have to do is find the right property—and others will pay for it.

> **JIM:** Really? That sounds good, but what about all the ongoing costs, like maintenance,

property taxes, insurance, HOA dues, et cetera?

ADVISOR: Don't worry. Others will pay for it.

JIM: So who are these "others"?

ADVISOR: They're your new tenants (we'll call them "owners"). You'll give them a lease for life (we'll call it a "contract" and give them a deed), and in return, they'll cover all your risks and costs of ownership. On top of that, they'll pay you the rent (retirement income) you need, with annual increases in perpetuity—and the rent is guaranteed by contract. All you have to do, like any landlord, is keep your tenants happy.

JIM: Where do I find such tenants?!

ADVISOR: Don't worry. We'll hire a team of recruiters to find them—and the tenants will even pay for this.

So you can have this pension, but it's not as free and easy as it may seem; you'll have to do some preliminary work to set it all up.

First, you'll need to have some legal work done to create the proper documents to satisfy regulators, and in conjunction, develop a "retirement" business plan . . . and then you'll need to start the registration process with the state and/or local jurisdiction(s) in which you plan to operate the business.

Next, you'll locate and buy an upscale, properly-zoned $10 million (or so) property that will fetch rent of about 5-6 percent of its value.

But since you have no spare money, you'll use your retirement business plan, together with a cosigner (an experienced real estate developer), to secure a bridge loan large enough to subdivide and improve your property as needed and to pay recruiters.

You then pay cash for the property and squirrel away the excess.

The lease (contract) will require your tenants (owners) to pay, let's say, 10 percent of the loan amount for the privilege of using the property for their lifetime (we'll call it a membership fee).

The good news for your tenants is that this membership fee must only be paid once—so they can easily pass usage rights on to their heirs with no such additional fee.

You then find nine other tenants under the same terms and pay off the bulk of your loan (with the remainder to be paid with project cash flow). They each get a month per year to use and enjoy this magnificent property, leaving two months for maintenance and repairs, which, of course, they agree to pay.

And what's best, your business plan allows you to hire lawyers and a professional management team to coordinate all this, from document preparation to hands-on maintenance to reservations, etc., all paid for by tenants.

Moreover, you can hire a hospitality and housekeeping team (plus any other amenities upon which you all agree)—and again, your tenants will pay for all this.

JIM: Whoa! So let me get this straight:

- I own the property, but they pay all costs of ownership, right? [Yep, you got that right.]

- They only own the rights to use it, right? [Yep.]

- They have the obligation to keep paying me rent whether they use it or not. Is that right? [YES.]

- And the rent will keep rising each year as I dictate, and they (or their heirs) will have the obligation to pay it to me or my heirs, right?

ADVISOR: That's right—or for as long as you mutually agree. Best of all, it's guaranteed by contract.

JIM: WHAT A SWEET DEAL!

Please note: The preceding is a story involving a hypothetical financial advisor and a client who is seeking a way to boost his retirement income. It is neither to be relied upon as financial advice nor as an inducement to invest in ownership of a timeshare project, but rather to illustrate, from my perspective, the benefits of owning a timeshare business that is a going concern, i.e., operating as described in the underlying documents. Conclusions drawn are based on my understanding of the provisions contained in typical timeshare documents.

Chapter 6

A LOOK AT THE TIMESHARE BUSINESS MODEL FROM THE CONSUMER'S PERSPECTIVE

Now, of course, there's the flip side to the timeshare business model—that of the owners, members, and tenants (OMTs). In the abstract, from a consumer perspective, timeshare purchases make little sense. Critics would recite the oft-heard complaint: why pay so much for something you can get at far less cost by paying for it as you go and on a pace of your choosing?

That makes sense but shows little appreciation of the contribution timeshares make to the lifestyle of those tenants truly suitable in both finances and temperament. They see a standard of quality well beyond that obtained with ad hoc arrangements or even with owning a vacation home of their own outright.

How do you know if you're the timeshare type? Give yourself one point for every "a," two points for every "b," and zero points for every "c."

1. What's the best present you could imagine receiving?

    a. A photo of your grandkids fishing off the same small dock where you learned to fish, just like your father before you

    b. An around-the-world plane ticket

    c. Peace and quiet

2. Your winning lotto number hits on the day you're closing on your vacation home—what's the first thing you buy?

    a. Flood insurance

    b. Another vacation home!

c. Someone to handle all this closing paper-work.

3. Your phone rings, and your heart skips a beat with excitement when you see the caller ID. Who is it, and what is it about?

a. Your contractor, who has been pricing out the custom creation you've been dreaming up. Sure, a volcanic rock climbing wall isn't for everyone, but you know exactly what you want, and you're willing to pay dearly for it.

b. Your guy-who-can-hook-you-up-with-anything, who's always tempting you with a new adventure. From obscure foods to hidden golf courses, even though they're often pricey, you love that he brings you in on experiences you don't have the time to look into for yourself.

c. Your boss—cancel the dinner plans and prepare for an all-nighter, you're finally going to crack this problem wide open!

4. The most special part about getting away from it all is . . .

    a. Painstakingly building your utopia

    b. The new adventures you have

    c. Going home

5. When you and your spouse talk about the possibility of buying a vacation home . . .

    a. Both of you like the idea of having a vacation property your family can enjoy for generations, and you are both confident that in the absence of the other, there would be no issues affording the expenses and performing the necessary maintenance.

    b. Both of you like the idea of having a vacation property that your family can enjoy for generations, but you're concerned with the nuisance and expense of managing and caring for it year-round.

c. One or neither of you want the trouble and expense of owning a vacation property.

Scored zero to three points? Home is where your heart is—book your vacations carefully and with good cancellation insurance, and don't even dream of time-shares; you just won't enjoy the emotional benefits. If you scored four to seven points, you're not looking for the key-ready experience of timeshares either—full ownership is important to you, and the headaches are offset with the ability to control your home away from home. Only those scoring eight to ten points can fully appreciate the timeshare experience!

Nonetheless, even high scorers can agree that time-shares come with some obvious financial concerns. In the main, they are two-fold: (1) their illiquidity and (2) their relatively high costs, especially the lifetime costs for the average consumer—neither of which are adequately disclosed at time of sale, based on my experience.

In order for this retired financial advisor to support a client's decision to buy a timeshare, that client should:

· Be able to pay cash for the timeshare to avoid having to rely on a so-called "mortgage loan" with unusually high rates from the developer;

- Have access to a guaranteed stream of income sufficient to cover annual maintenance fees with expected increases over time to meet or exceed the fee increases or 5 percent, whichever is higher.

Based on those, few would qualify. But that doesn't make timeshares bad. It just means that, from my perspective, timeshares in their current form are being oversold to the public.

So how do we proceed?

It's simple. There must be both proper disclosure and some form of financial underwriting.

Timeshare offerings usually include a bold (routinely ignored) statement at the beginning of the disclosures that, for a variety of reasons, a timeshare purchase involves *risk*. The risk is the loss of funds—funds that might otherwise be needed for any number of planned or unplanned life events, like unemployment, uninsured medical bills, a long-term disability, long-term healthcare costs, et cetera—or even funds that you just want to use for other purposes. Either way, loss of these funds into a timeshare presents risk. So in addition to having the means to pay for a timeshare and its ongoing fees, a tenant should also be in a position to pay for other life events, like educational costs for children, a secure retirement, et cetera.

As an aside, in the world of life insurance contracts, many include an optional provision called "disability waiver of premium." This means that in the event an insured becomes disabled, as defined in the contract, while that contract is in force, the premium (payment) normally required is <u>waived</u> by the insurance company. While there's certainly an added cost for this, it is a very important benefit. Since the purchase of timeshares always involves *risk*, is there any reason why the industry should not offer some kind of waiver of maintenance fee in the event something untoward happens to the owner? It's just a thought, but something that should be considered by those undertaking any meaningful timeshare industry reform.

In my opinion, the timeshare industry must adopt (or be compelled to adopt) a far more rigorous set of standards before responsibly selling their products to consumers. The financial services industry has long had standards of compliance imposed upon it. These standards don't just appear in writing, they are actively enforced by both those within the industry and without. In other words, it's a serious endeavor. Shown below are a couple of samples appearing in a recent publication serving professionals in that industry. Both are abstracts of articles appearing therein.

The first applies to the life insurance industry regarding policy disclosure, and reads like this:

According to the rules of fair economic competition, financial markets can only work properly when consumers and product salespeople (agents) are appropriately informed. This article proposes a format for the presentation of effective and appropriate disclosure of material information about any type of life insurance policy. Broadly speaking, disclosure of a life insurance policy involves addressing the following conceptual matters: guarantees, uncertainty, and participation, various tax and "structural" aspects, policy operational mechanics and measurements, and policyholder choices and their implications. The five fundamental cost components of any life insurance policy (six, if investment management costs are separated from administrative costs) are: sales, claims, administration, premium taxes, and capital charges. Policies with investment components require additional disclosures (i.e., returns, portfolio characteristics, et cetera) and an explanation of their tax privileges' ramifications. Additional disclosure-related aspects are discussed. The possible impacts of the proposed disclosure format upon the industry's past, present, and future operations are also explored.[1]

The second applies to the life insurance industry as it pertains to a New York State regulation and reads:

Regulation 187 governs the behavior of New York life insurance and annuity producers (agents) when making recommendations with respect to a life insurance or annuity policy owned or being purchased by a New

---

1 Fechtel, R. Brian and Connel Fullenkamp, "Life Insurance Policy Disclosure for the 21st Century," *Journal of Financial Service Professionals* 75, no. 1 (January 2021): 36-58.

York consumer. Its purpose is to prevent acts or practices that are deceptive or unfair. A close reading of the regulation reveals many similarities to the Securities and Exchange Commission's (SEC) new Regulation Best Interest. Both require the individual making the recommendation to act in the "best interest" of the consumer. Both impose increased record-keeping requirements. Both emphasize principles-based selling practices.[2]

The purpose here is not to bore you with the details of the articles, but rather to demonstrate the degree to which regulators and those in supervision recognize the importance of disclosure in the sales process. Since timeshare marketing is also subject to acts that might be considered deceptive and/or unfair, the industry should be held to similar standards.

Shifting now from compliance issues, if you're

---

2   Richards, Douglas B., "How to Become a Consumer-Centric, Process-Oriented Closer under New York's Regulation 187," *Journal of Financial Service Professionals* 75, no. 1 (January 2021): 25–27.

intrigued with the possibly of owning a timeshare business for yourself—if you want to try making some modest (or perhaps, like Jim, some not-so-modest) profits from timeshares while enjoying their benefits, consider this approach: pick out an existing timeshare project, one that you'd really like to enjoy as an owner if money were no object. Make a study of it and, assuming they're offering sales presentations, go to one—*but do not buy*. Stay long enough to learn what you must about the project, especially if there are any restrictions about renting it out to others when you're unable to use it yourself. Since you can't count on any oral representations from salespeople (an issue we will discuss further later in this book), ask to see proof in the project documents.

Once satisfied short-term rentals are permitted, politely exit the meeting and search "for sale" offerings of that project on the secondary market. Here, you may be able to buy the same or a similar timeshare unit as that shown you by the salesperson—but for pennies on the dollar. Search online for reputable marketing services that may help you offer your timeshare to the public as a short-term rental. For a fee, you should be able to get any required training and then have them "manage" the rental process for you from A to Z.

Once satisfied, buy the desired timeshare on the secondary market, enter into an agreement with your manager, and rent it for enough to accomplish three things: (1) recoup your annual maintenance fee and overhead costs; (2) make whatever profit the rental market will allow; all the while (3) possibly enjoying the use of your "ideal" timeshare yourself.

Though the financial model for timeshares distinctly benefits the industry, a smart, well-positioned consumer can enjoy both the financial and creature-comfort benefits of these incredible properties today—even before the desperately-needed reforms we'll be discussing next.

Chapter 7

REFORMING THE TIMESHARE INDUSTRY

In my quest to better understand the timeshare industry, I've gone where few owners have, examining the underlying documents and pressing against the doors that separate the banquet from the kitchen. I've even gone beyond the beaten path of many timeshare industry executives, who, in their day-to-day work, seem to accept the fact that "they are what they are" and rather mindlessly follow a script that's perfectly natural to them.

Part of gathering input for this book was to collect a few stories of individual timeshare owners who are delighted with their experiences (there are many).

It occurred to me that one of the long-tenured and much beloved staff members (let's call him Bob) at the Old Guard, where I was then staying, would be a great source for leads. After all, most owners know him, and he shares great rapport with them.

I thought my request was innocent enough: I gave him a couple of pages describing the project and asked him to give me his best, most vivid recollections of two or three delighted owners, so I would never need to directly intrude on their vacations. I clearly marked on the handout that the book would neither reveal the names of timeshares nor owners. And, to make it easy, I suggested he just provide oral input as I took notes. We agreed, and I asked him to give it some thought; we'd meet again in a couple of days to discuss.

Well, he certainly presented input—but not at all what I sought!

Although he didn't say it, my interpretation of his response was that protocol required him to report me as potential trouble to his superiors. Consequently, the first thing he told me during our next brief meeting was that he would not be able to help.

I found the news troubling but insightful. Of course, he wasn't permitted to speak any further about it, so no additional words passed between us. But it all seemed so strange that I resolved to learn more from the source.

A bit later that very morning, I wound up speaking with a junior member of the management team. In sum, he told me they couldn't help. Instead, he suggested I talk directly with owners to get my input. I thought it fair enough, so I quietly seated myself in the club's lobby and began respectfully approaching other owners as they wandered past.

Soon after I began chatting amicably with one woman, another employee, dressed in a black suit, walked up, pointed sternly at me, and ordered me to come her way. I assumed she was the boss and said as much. But she quickly corrected that impression to let me know, in no uncertain terms, that she was head of security.

Standing in the lobby, she began talking to me before another person, a man I assumed to be the "big boss," flew out of nowhere and into my face, challenging my very presence in the Old Guard. Visibly enraged, he was unaware that I was both an owner and staying there (penthouse, no less). But even after being alerted to my own position, he didn't seem to care; his rage continued.

All levels of management seemed keenly aware that I was writing a book, and obviously, they didn't approve. Their resistance was intense. It's fair to say that I was rather severely admonished. The whole scene was very strange indeed, especially considering it played out in the main lobby, in plain view of employees and guests alike.

I was prohibited from "soliciting" (for my book) on the premises. Perhaps this was understandable. Nonetheless, in my view, the whole incident was vastly overplayed, but it provided more feedback than I had ever imagined!

Obviously, they don't like sunlight.

The Industries Surrounding the Timeshare Industry

It has been said that all politics are local, and just as there are plenty of critics of timeshares, there are plenty of scavengers eager to jump in and fill the voids that might exist. They know there's a market for anti-timeshare services. Having accepted the fact that timeshares are what they are and cannot be changed (after all, they're legal, right?), the "Exit Timeshare Industry" is alive and well. In fact, I've come to see it as its own thriving timeshare sub-industry, dependent on the motherlode. Within those symbiotic industries, there are legions of solicitors poised to help dissatisfied owners get out of timeshares. Their appeal is simple: it's you and me against the monster! Yet the timeshare industry "monster" seems to tolerate them as it, nonetheless, opposes them on behalf of consumers.

As research for this book and at the suggestion of my spouse (who felt it may be time to rid ourselves of our timeshare at the Old Guard, particularly after my experience in the lobby), we booked an appointment with one particular timeshare exit company. Chosen based on the TV endorsement of a high-profile personality, as far as I was concerned, it was as good as any. The head office for the operation was somewhere on the West Coast, but since they had a rep in my area, we set up a meeting.

From the appearance of his shared office and work environment, the rep seemed to be a part-timer whose job was, understandably, to quickly engage us for their services. The document checklist sent to us by the head office seemed complete, but our rep had little interest in it. Instead, he focused on one thing: our last maintenance fee invoice.

He entered the Old Guard property name and fee amount into his proprietary software to produce what I had sought: their fee (about 150 percent of the annual maintenance fee) for getting us out. Of course, since the process is "proprietary," we were neither told what their fee would cover nor anything substantial about the work that might be involved. We were left with the impression that it was none of our business. Like a typical timeshare presentation, this mirror experience was about emotion. It was left to one's imagination what actually happens in the exit-timeshare sausage factory, and to what legal effect.

Afterward, I found a timeshare exit company that said they'd charge a flat fee (less than half of the first company's fee) for their service, regardless the maintenance fee paid. Because the video promotion used the word "guarantee" liberally, I wanted to know what was and was not guaranteed in the contract. When I asked for a copy before committing, they declined to provide it.

Apart from "exiting" a timeshare, there are other services within this subset industry to rid owners of ongoing maintenance fees. Many do it by helping owners sell their timeshare. I've had a couple of interactions with these; neither proposed a fee anywhere near that of the timeshare exit companies (though neither provided adequate assurance of results, either). Again, one is left to ponder the effectiveness of what they purport to do. Suffice to say, we did not engage them. As I've come to learn, when the time comes to rid ourselves of one or more timeshare(s), we (or our representative) will first go back to the organization from which we purchased. When and if that time comes, it will likely be for rather compelling reasons (family death, permanent disability, et cetera), in which case most reputable timeshares (and there are some) will take back the ownership interest without a fee.

In speaking with many of those solicitors (timeshare resale, timeshare exit, timeshare cancellation, timeshare attorneys, et cetera), all of whom compete with each other, the theme was consistent and basically echoes their sales pitch: "It's good that you found me because . . ."; "We're unique because . . ."; "The timeshare industry is hopelessly corrupt, and there's no way out except through my proprietary service . . ."; "You know it's the right thing to do because XYZ endorses me . . ."; "So let's get to work." Understandably, despite the veneer of empathy, none have any interest beyond bashing the timeshare industry and closing today's deal. Their view can be expressed thusly: *Everyone knows what it is, and knows it can't be changed. Just because . . . learn to live with it. Sorry you've fallen prey to them, but we're here to provide a lifeline to you and others. We're a noble service to humanity! Here's our hefty invoice.*

Sadly, it also appears that none have given the first thought to improving the timeshare industry itself. But then, why should they? It's not their problem. Besides, it's contrary to their interests. My interactions with them made it abundantly clear that they were no more interested in my mission—to create a better, more functional, thriving, and non-exploitative timeshare model to benefit owners and timeshare opportunities alike—than the timeshare industry itself.

American Resort Development Association (ARDA)

Like virtually all industries, timeshares have trade association representation in Washington, DC. But since the timeshare industry is not regulated at the federal level, it intrigued me why they had such a significant presence there. As I began running into roadblocks very quickly in my initial dialog with the developer of the Gilded Enigma, I decided to take a two-pronged approach to voice my concerns and get my questions answered. Surely, either my own timeshare or the American Resort Development Association (ARDA), who politicks on behalf of the entire wider endeavor, would see the wisdom in conversing with me as a committed, interested, and passionate advocate for their cause. Based on my experiences, I was starting to seriously consider writing a book on timeshares, and I thought ARDA might be interested in knowing what I was doing.

Don't laugh.

I sent an email to ARDA on March 25, 2019, copying in the GE for transparency, which read in part:

> I read with interest your recent update, *Large Timeshare Exit Companies Oppose Legislation that Protects Consumers*, and found it quite informative. As the timeshare industry works to oppose the opposition, it further stimulates my interest in helping defend the industry in a serious and responsible way.

I'm a retired financial services guy who earned the educational credentials held dear by the profession. I mainly worked in the areas of cash flow modeling, philanthropy, and estate distribution planning. I am also a real estate investor. Leading up to retirement, I discovered the pleasure of acquiring and enjoying multiple timeshare interests. You might say I was the ideal prospect.

My youngest brother, however, who is also in financial services, has a completely different view of the industry, largely driven by reputation. This mild family tension inspires me to present timeshares from what I see as a more enlightened perspective, documenting the interests of both industry and consumer to make clear something I believe to be true—the industry operates the way it does for good and worthwhile reasons.

Please don't get me wrong. My experience tells me the industry has plenty of room to improve, even among its biggest players. But this is neither unique to the industry nor irreversible. In my opinion, the improvements are simple—but not easy. However, once achieved, they would go a long way toward improving public image and further increasing sales.

While there are many books on the subject, it seems most are decidedly negative. Some are not, but [their] content is usually limited to ways to beat the system, et cetera. And beyond "puff pieces" written by the industry, there are no books of any substance that actually endorse timeshares.

If the facts support it, I propose to change that.

In order to be a "going concern," any business must first obtain capital to open its doors and then generate a predictable, positive cash flow from satisfied customers. This is as true of the timeshare industry as any other.

As envisioned, my intent is to present a full story by explaining the timeshare business model as I understand it and why it exists. I have my opinion about the model, but players within the industry are reluctant to discuss. Here is where ARDA may be able to provide some clarity.

In the belief that a well-educated consumer is the industry's best customer, it would state the facts in a dispassionate way. And while it would reaffirm the truism of "no free lunch," it would also seek to demonstrate the tremendous upside potential for those properly screened and for whom timeshares are suitable.

In the process, I wish to shed some friendly light on an industry that seems to be an enigma and, as warranted, suggest opportunities for improvement.

I note the pricey membership levels shown on your website. Of course, it confirms that ARDA caters to the industry, not individuals. I understand. Nonetheless, I would like to share some thoughts, from a customer's perspective, in support of that industry—and ARDA may be able to help.

Thus, I propose a meeting with you, your boss, and perhaps other ARDA official(s) to discuss the project and get your feedback. To be fair, I expect to consult with those in the timeshare exit business as well to get their perspective. So, as you check your cal-

endar, allow me to suggest we meet sometime after April 15th.

Of course, you guessed right. Like all aspects of the
industry, they seemed bound to a code of silence.

When my letter was met by that now all-too-pre-
dictable silence, I thought, *What's to lose, they're local.*
Why not just pay them a visit to see how it goes? What's
the worst that can happen, right?

And so, the day came, and I walked into the lobby
of the building housing the ARDA. I announced
my presence at building security and told them
that while I had no appointment, I'd like to visit the
ARDA offices to establish a dialogue about a project
I was working on. Although dubious, the guards said
I might be in luck, as a gentleman from ARDA was
there with them in the main lobby. We met briefly,
and as he apparently detected no malice on my part,
he invited me to accompany him up to the offices.
Seated just inside ARDA's lobby, he screened me
further. I gave him more background and mentioned
the name of the staff member I had written, asking
if he might be available to, at least, meet briefly to
exchange greetings.

The mood quickly changed. He told me that would

not be possible, but that ARDA had an office in Orlando, Florida to deal with individuals like me. He said this was not the place. I left with only a name and number for an individual in Florida for their Resort Owners Coalition (ARDA-ROC), along with the impression that, for what it's worth, the ARDA lobby is nice.

I called the individual in Florida and left a detailed voice mail. In due course, a man returned the call with a perfunctory voice mail lacking any sense of engagement or purpose. This was obviously a dead-end.

The pattern was becoming familiar. As a result, I came to see such presence as a façade to show those who may care that, yes, ARDA-ROC does have a "customer service" function. But is ARDA-ROC really interested in customers? I think not. Rather, it, and the whole of ARDA, seem to exist for the benefit of major players in the industry, each of which pays a substantial fee each year for their lobbying efforts. Who pays the lobbyists? Is it the major timeshare players? It would make sense.

In other words, it's a typical lobbying operation. It seems the lobbying efforts of each state are centrally coordinated at ARDA headquarters, though the fact that there are no industry regulators in DC continues to beg the question of why they're located there—but, I guess, why not? They have to be somewhere, and who knows? There may well be those with influence in DC.

So I've concluded that timeshares are actually "regulated" at the state level in what seems to be a rather cozy relationship where the industry writes governing documents (what's new?) unique to that jurisdiction and the respective legislatures largely approve them as written. While the states (no doubt aided by the industry) lay out exacting standards for businesses to operate as timeshares within their jurisdiction, they appear to make no attempt to supervise those operations once in place. Thus, one is left to conclude there is no real supervision of timeshare operations within their jurisdictions; the industry is effectively self-regulated.

From what I can tell, ARDA is in the public relations business (like other trade associations) and does what it must on behalf of their members to keep a wide array of local legislators happy and satisfied.

On the federal level, the Federal Trade Commission (FTC) provides very broad guidance regarding timeshares but makes no attempt to supervise or regulate their operations. Essentially, once the purchase is made and a consumer has a complaint, it's up to the individual to prove his or her case with timeshare officials. The best those officials appear to do is to provide a (largely ineffective) complaint line.

Stories of timeshare abuse are widespread. Yet, odd as it seems, when the Consumer Financial Protection Bureau (CFPB) was launched in 2011, its reach did not extend to the industry. Instead, it was created to protect consumers from certain financial-industry practices related to mortgages, student loans, credit cards, etc. At the time, and perhaps by design, timeshares were not seen as being part of financial services. They still aren't. Perhaps this is why the industry has its own system of "mortgage loans" for prospective owners needing them.

CFPB aside, the solution is not to create some kind of massive federal oversight regime. Instead, a good start would be to adopt something simple and industry-wide. If so many (if not all) players are against reform, we should ask why.

One might surmise the obvious: follow the money. Doing so would likely reveal the extent to which corporate and individual wealth, success, and livelihood (owners including stockholders, corporate executives, salespersons, corporate employees, et cetera) depend upon maintaining the industry's status quo. But one thing seems clear to me: it's an industry with a business model built on a false premise.

While there are many opportunities for improvement, that false premise is embodied by one. It's a stipulation in most timeshare sales contracts that reads something like this: the consumer (the very reason for the industry's success) understands (well after making a purchase decision) that their decision is based solely on the purchase agreement and loan documents together with the governing documents of the project, which (they're advised) contain all the terms and conditions of their ownership—*and that they should not rely upon any oral presentations as the basis for their purchase.*

But in many cases, that's simply not true: consumers are required to attest to this in writing at closing, well <u>after</u> they've made their buying decision and well <u>before</u> they are able see (if ever) the documents upon which, it's assumed, they've based their decision. Thus, as a practical matter, consumers have <u>no</u> basis upon which to make their decision <u>except</u> for an oral presentation. The creation of this scurrilous "evidence" to the contrary seems particularly egregious.

And so, like the businesses surrounding them, the timeshare industry itself seems to view its reality as: *everyone knows what it is and knows it can't be changed. Just because. Learn to live with it.*

But must we? The answer is clearly *no*. It's been said that timeshares are a legal scam. If so, why are they legal in view of their established, but unwritten, sales practices? And what should we do about it?

Based on my experience, I view the industry as a formidable assemblage with legal moats attempting to appear as a model citizen in the marketplace, while inwardly a reclusive, self-regulated force bent on maintaining power, control, and its ability to efficiently capture new and "upgrading" consumers in the relentless pursuit of growth. The industry is blind (or chooses to be) on its negative effects on consumers.

If we, the suitable, committed, eager OMTs are to reform the timeshare industry, draw more people into the possibilities of the model in the way it should operate, and move this fascinating experiment in "owning a vacation" toward what it could optimally be, we cannot look to the exit or lobbying forces to assist us. As you will see, my proposals for reform are clear and simple, and it will be up to us, together, to see that they are made.

Chapter 8

TUGGING AT THE CURTAIN

An Introduction to a Problem (Which Probably Needs No Introduction)

Imagine this . . . you arrived in New York City yesterday, enjoyed an evening on the town, got a refreshing night's sleep in your luxurious suite, then arrived early and excited the next morning to the presentation you'd been invited to hear—best of all, you'd get some free tickets to a Broadway show just to be there. What's not to like?

You were greeted by friendly staff, and after

a wait that seemed long, you met your sales representative. All was cordial, and after some small talk, they began to present the lifestyle that awaited you if you decided to make this part of your future. And once you have it, no one could ever take it away from you.

It sounded good and seemed relatively simple. All you had to do was pay an up-front fee (your rep was able to get a small discount for you). It was sort of like making a down payment on a home, then paying HOA dues. But instead of buying an entire home, you would only pay for what you want and need. As they said, buying one piece of the pizza instead of the entire pizza (or pizza store) seemed a smart way to buy a vacation "home."

Your rep seemed especially good at carving out the best deal for you (probably better than others), getting you the most for monies paid. Although you were told the presentation would only last about an hour and a half, once you learned about the opportunity, you had no problem taking whatever time might be necessary to secure this deal.

An hour and a half became several hours and eventually, the closing paperwork was ready. You thought to yourself, *Maybe we can still make the 7:00 performance at Lincoln Center . . .*

When you finally got to closing, it all seemed so blurred. You just wanted to get it done.

In the end, you were congratulated, given a package of the papers, went back to your suite and collapsed. They said something about a rescission provision or period. Whatever, you guessed they had to say that, but who cares? You're glad you did it.

The next morning after coffee and breakfast, you take a closer look. After flipping through many documents, one stands out—something called the "Statement of Understanding of Vacation Ownership Interest" (or something similar). Of course, you had initialed and signed where asked, even the part that is now starting to concern you—but in view of everything, you're sure everything is fine and there's no issue . . .

Now, you begin to focus on it, and it says: "The Purchase Agreement and loan documents together with the governing documents of the Project contain all the terms and conditions of your ownership . . ."

Of course, you never talked about any of this. After closing, you were given a copy of the purchase agreement and loan documents, even though you don't plan to actually use a loan. But what about the governing documents of the project—what and where are they?

You realize that the only useful and understandable information you got before making a buying decision came from your sales rep—where else would you get it? And you think, *Surely they wouldn't steer me wrong . . .*

But then, the Statement of Ownership goes on to the worst part: "You should not rely upon any oral representations as the basis for your purchase."

So where does that leave us? You think, *What's going on here?* You then realize you had nothing *but* oral representation to use as basis!

But you still believe your decision was well-founded. After all, you don't want to embarrass yourself or others, so you decide to just let it slide. But then again, you start to speculate over what you missed, like where the governing documents are. Sadly, life takes over and you never follow up.

Some important points:

- I believe this story should never happen at a timeshare presentation. What has happened in this example is not uncommon. It's very serious and an intentional error of omission.

- But from the customer's perspective, he has just told the world, and the timeshare has it on record, that by his agreement, he understood and agreed with the "terms and conditions of his ownership." He feels helpless but wants to believe everything is alright.

- The kabuki dance starts as all parties begin to play their roles and avoid the topic. The sales rep and staff are so proud of the customer and his wise decision that he starts to mirror their comportment. Pleasant smiles and happy small talk rule the day—with anything contrary shunned by all.

- During this period, the customer is still trying to defend his decision, disinclined to rock the boat by pursuing rescission or even complaining . . .

- Because the timeshare company has conditioned them to it, most sales reps believe, "Oh, they know all this, what's the big deal?"

- I respectfully disagree. The newbies certainly don't know this! Even existing owners' memories tend to fade over time, as they (and their families) unwittingly continue to be "tenants for life."

- Some in management have said my recommendation to be entirely transparent is totally impractical, going on to say, "There's no way an hour and a half presentation can possibly take the time to cover so much detail." With this, I agree.

- The IMPORTANT MESSAGE I have drafted below is suggested for use in these presentations, intended to inform and/or remind customers upfront of essential characteristics of timeshares, and to do so without unduly disrupting the company's sales rhythm. As a one-page document, customers can read and understand it in just a few minutes.

- Should it, as some might contend, threaten to "kill the deal," that's actually a good aspect. If the sales rep sees customer concern, they can courteously flesh it out immediately and perhaps save everyone's time. Afterward, the rep either goes on with presentation or courteously ends it. Either way would be a perfectly fine outcome—one that would be fair, open, and honest.

- If done right, I contend such action would increase sales, certainly in the long-term, because it's the right thing to do and part of being professional.

IMPORTANT MESSAGE

Thanks for attending this sales presentation. We want you to get the most out of it and respect your time. In presenting the many advantages of ownership, our sales professionals may not have time to go over all ownership details. This provides a few of them that our existing owners believe important for you to know and understand as you consider joining them. Please refer to project documents for full details. Thanks again for your interest.

- Caveat Emptor: You should not rely upon any oral representations as the basis for your purchase. Instead, you should consult the Purchase Agreement and any loan documents together with the governing documents of the Project, which contain all the terms and conditions of your ownership.

- Prices Negotiable: Prices shown by your sales professional are based on those found in the project documents. However, they are negotiable.

- Ongoing Fee: In addition to purchase price and closing costs, you will pay an annual maintenance fee of about 2 to 3 percent of purchase price. This fee will likely increase over time. It is due at the beginning of the first calendar year and will continue each year for the duration of your ownership interest.

- Not a Real Estate Investment: Purchase of a Vacation Ownership Interest is a lifestyle decision. It should be based on its value as a vacation experience, not a real estate investment. This is because, generally, there is no established market for resale interests and any resale value is uncertain. Think of it as illiquid.

- Real Estate Taxes: Notwithstanding above, such purchase is considered a real estate interest for which you receive a deed stating such. Hence, you will be responsible for paying real estate taxes as part of your annual maintenance fee.

- Financing: If your purchase is financed with the seller, you will pay an unusually high interest rate to help compensate seller's added risk as there is no other established market for such notes.

After many unanswered letters to Dean, his boss, Adam, and then to the president, CEO, and director of the corporation from which Midtown Modernity and Gilded Enigma's parent company had spun off, I sent this piece as an addendum to the letter below—which, while long even in this abbreviated version, contains several kernels of reforms that could make the entire timeshare enterprise everything it should be.

> When I see something that is clearly wrong and affects large numbers of people, I must speak out. This is such a time. Recent experience tells me the Gilded Enigma, its Parent Corporation, and, by implication, your corporation itself must improve at least one aspect of its sales practice. I'm writing to explain and propose a solution.
>
> And while this letter addresses a relatively small and fixable issue, it suggests something

broader: your corporate culture, through the Gilded Enigma, may be unduly influenced by the timeshare industry. This is written because your senior executives have shown little to no interest in change. Perhaps the following underscores.

As a courtesy, Dean, the Gilded Enigma manager, was copied on my communication to the American Resort Development Association (ARDA) in late March. In it, I speculated on writing a book, inter alia. It was circulated within the Parent Corporation, and got to Adam, a senior executive who made a personal declaration to me three days later in NYC at the initial HOA Board meeting. In no uncertain terms, he vowed he would neither answer my letter sent earlier nor "help [me] write a book." I didn't ask for help and thought his assertion rather odd.

With that, my name is W.H. Campbell. I've been a loyal customer of your corporation since 2007 and engaged Parent Corporation member since April 2016.

As the Wizard told Dorothy in *The Wizard of Oz* when Toto yanked away the curtain,

"Pay no attention to that man behind the curtain . . . I am the great and powerful Oz!" Like her, I've seen behind the curtain—and must act.

As before with the Gilded Enigma, I'm writing to propose an improvement to correct a glaring omission in the sales process, one involving lack of timely disclosure to customers. Correction is needed to adequately serve the public by providing them with a fair and compliant sales presentation with documents.

In reflecting on timeshares and recent experience with your corporation, I've asked myself questions like who or what, beyond small staffs in state offices, actually supervises and/or regulates the industry? What does ARDA really do? How much of it is on behalf of consumers (little, I think) as opposed to the industry? With whom do they lobby since, as I understand, the industry is regulated at the state level? If regulation is as weak as suspected, are there any ethical standards?

In affiliating with your corporation, I was no stranger to the timeshare concept, having owned vacation interests elsewhere, including one in Midtown Manhattan since 1997. Upon adding your properties to my portfolio, I became more interested in the business aspects of timeshares and find what I've discovered in the documents to be fascinating.

As with prior timeshares, I've been attracted to them because I liked them, could afford them, and was able to quickly complete the transaction. Despite comments herein, I continue as a satisfied member of all. You might say I was the ideal prospect. I gave no time to any documents. Why, then, am I concerned?

It's because so few are ideal prospects. Even with me, mild concerns started with Midtown Modernity's relatively high acquisition costs, which, in turn, spurred greater interest in the underlying business model.

But the real concerns started in January 2019 and continue to this day. You see, while I had never been particularly interested in documents, I came to realize that I was not alone. In fact, it seems no one else (including management) is very interested, either. So, the project documents sit there in the background while business operations flow more or less independent of them. But something is wrong.

And that's because documents are primarily designed to inform and protect the public's interest. When certain provisions are ignored for expedience or short-term business gains to the detriment of the consuming public, something is seriously wrong. Thus, my recommendations are designed to correct one flaw in the sales process to provide essential transparency.

Yes, I've become somewhat of a zealot when it comes to timeshares. As you might surmise, it came about while studying project documents of the Gilded Enigma, especially the Management Agreement. That's when I saw behind the curtain, if you will, and discovered the enormous profitability of them. But are these ill-gained profits? Maybe, but that's debatable.

As I see it, the first "wrong" at your timeshares, like timeshares in general, is lack of candor and disclosure. Beyond that, I believe my total experience, both good and bad, may be of value to other owners and prospective timeshare owners alike as they engage this insular industry, which some critics call a "legal scam." More can be provided on that later, should there be interest.

But for now, I appeal to your business interest in tightening up the sales process to make it worthy of your corporate brand— and a model for the industry to emulate. My suggestions will be a good start.

Thanks for your leadership of your corporate brand, and for your interest in this opportunity for improvement.

I never received a response.

There is likely much more to follow, as those daring to dig further into this "riddle wrapped in a mystery inside an enigma" may find. But the very first step in this long process is to unmask the unspoken. This is part of that effort.

Meanwhile, wherever you are in the timesharing experience, enjoy the banquet—but be wary of the sausage factory. For the suitable buyer, timeshares

may be better than you think, but reread this book—
and all of the relevant project documents—formulate
your questions, demand the answers, and determine
your suitability before buying one!

EPILOGUE

In the midst of my search for answers within the timeshare industry, the world has been thrown into further complication with the COVID-19 experience. The hospitality industry, like many others, has been devastated; within that, however, the timeshare industry has been far less affected. Though not immune to the effects, the timeshare industry has still collected its recurring revenue streams from contractually-bound OMTs, even while we are unable to utilize these vacations we own.

As with other industries with which I have interacted as a consumer during this time, our timeshares have made previously-unimaginable concessions— though mostly in terms of booking flexibility. Visiting our North Carolina timeshare in November 2020, we found the contactless check-in smooth and simple; though we missed interacting with the staff and other visitors, it was a wonderful trip and a bright spot in a difficult year for all. I have been unable to visit my two New York timeshares, as Midtown Manhattan was an early epicenter of the infection and still faces enormous challenges today.

Of course, I do not blame the timeshare companies for these difficulties. As I began to receive offers, discounts, and incentives from other industries, encouraging me to continue interacting with them as they shifted their business models and found new ways to serve customers, though, I started to wonder what financial incentives I could expect from the timeshare companies. Having heard nothing by August 2020, I wrote a letter to the president and CEO of the corporation that controls the Gilded Enigma, which suggested, in part:

> Circumstances today provide an opportunity for us to connect on an issue of mutual interest.
> As the world knows, COVID-19 has had devastating effects on most

business enterprises, especially those within the hospitality industry. I can only imagine the enormous adverse effects on your corporation and many of its employees.

But timeshares operate under a completely different business model. And it's one I've studied with interest.

Whereas your hospitality corporation, writ large, deals within an "open" market environment, i.e., one involving customers with unfettered discretion, flexibility, and choice, the timeshare segment deals almost entirely with a "closed" market, i.e., one involving customers (members) bound by contract.

Because of this, the timeshares have a far more predicable cash flow and, one would assume, are able to continue to employ and fully compensate management and staff, pay any vendor amounts due, and comply with existing contractual obligations, et cetera. In other words, it's a disruption to the usual business rhythm, but otherwise little more than an inconvenience.

In fact, and for what it's worth, COVID-19 has actually presented opportunities for savings as a result of avoiding many variable expenses, things like housekeeping, food and beverage, laundry expenses, et cetera, as well as the opportunity to reduce our annual HOA reserve fund contribution for one year to reflect substantially less use.

Like many consumers, you've probably been granted a reduced cost, in the form of a rebate, for certain forms of insurance (auto, dental, etc.) where company exposure to risk has obviously been reduced.

In a similar vein, as a matter of fairness and to "compensate" those who pay for all this (the members) while getting little benefit, it only makes sense to do something unknown in the timeshare industry: instead of announcing another increase to the annual maintenance fee, actually *reduce* it for 2021.

To my knowledge, members still have no board participation in management decisions. So please accept this as one member's input.

Like my other communications to the industry, this letter was met with silence. I did receive a voice mail from a deputy (Adam), asking that I call him to discuss. I wrote back:

Hi Adam,

In the midst of this heated political season, the phone rang earlier today as it often does and, as usual, I ignored it. Most who call are uninvited solicitors.

But upon playing the message, I was surprised to hear your voice asking me to call you about my letter to the president & CEO. Thank you.

My initial response was delight that he got it and, at least, thought it worthy of a response of some sort. I suppose your call was that response.

I remember your saying that you (and presumably others) don't respond in writing to six-page letters. Apparently, that includes two-page letters as well, even those addressing a specific issue.

So I'm herein politely acknowledging your call but with no intent to return it.

Instead, I would appreciate your having

staff draft something for you or the president and CEO that responds in a meaningful way to my question. To the extent you can share it, I would like to know corporate policy on such an unusual issue. I suspect others have already asked. If so, that would make it easy. If not, someone should have asked. It strikes me as a matter of basic fairness and, at least, worthy of a written response.

The cynic in me suspects there is no way maintenance fees could or would be adjusted downward. And indeed, there may be very good reasons. Knowing them would be helpful to owners as we try to more fully understand our relationship with the Gilded Enigma.

I look forward to your response. It would help me better understand the constraints under which the Gilded Enigma, and perhaps timeshares in general, operate. Thanks.

Of course, I never received a response. However, for what it's worth, the maintenance fee for 2021 was actually reduced. Perhaps some in the industry are starting to get the message.

That aside, it is further interesting to note that some in the timeshare industry have applied for and received public COVID-19 relief money through the US Government's Payroll Protection Program (PPP). One major timeshare corporation received and then had to return somewhere close to $70 million in PPP funds. At least two of the time-shares I have ownership interest in have received PPP funds; one, according to published reports, applied as a nonprofit organization and member of the "Fitness and Recreational Sports Centers" industry and obtained millions of dollars in support of five hundred jobs. While I can vouch for the existence of this fitness center, I have no idea how they would have supported anywhere near that number of jobs—or why my maintenance fees, which were collected and assumedly dispersed as usual, did not cover these positions.

It's unclear how widespread such claims by the timeshare industry have been. Regardless, for an industry already generously supported by its OMTs, it seems peculiar that they seek further public subsidies. This presents confusion, as it seems these bills have been double dropped and double paid. Obviously, there should be greater transparency into how these companies, which I implicitly endorse through my participation, are running their operations—which, I suppose, brings the message of this book full circle. Though the circumstances are unprecedented, the patterns are not. In good times and in bad, the timeshare industry needs to open the curtains and be exposed to the light.

If nothing else, this further underscores the need for industry reform.

Appendix 1
BOOK TIMELINE

<u>Spring 1997</u>: My wife and I accepted an invitation to visit the Old Guard—at the time, the only Midtown Manhattan property offering vacation ownership interests. Our weekend stay, complete with the enticements of Broadway tickets and dinner, ended in an ownership purchase of seven days per year.

<u>Fall 1997</u>: We stayed in the Old Guard as owners for the first time and loved it.

<u>2005</u>: We attended an Old Guard update and learned of the Penthouse Suites addition. Fresh from rewatching the Ric Burns's epic 17.5-hour documentary on the history of New York City, I think

it was the easiest sale I ever made to myself. Our enjoyment of our Old Guard timeshare ownership would now continue on an even grander scale.

2013: We visited Mountain Lodge in North Carolina and became acquainted with another type of timeshare, the equity-residence club. We added Mountain Lodge membership to our timeshare ownership portfolio, and it quickly became my wife's favorite.

Spring 2014: With my father's death in 2012, my three younger brothers and I resolved to have family reunions each spring. I hosted the second one at the Old Guard in 2014; based on our enjoyment of it as a family and my timeshare holdings, I became the go-to guy for finding suitable accommodations for each family reunion since.

April 13, 2016: My wife and I purchased ownership interest in Midtown Modernity.

October 2016: I first attempted to learn more about timeshare business models in general and Midtown Modernity in particular through their sales management, to no true avail.

<u>January 30, 2017</u>: We transferred interest from Midtown Modernity to the Gilded Enigma.

<u>November 2018</u>: I was again spurred to learn more about the business of the timeshare industry with the arrival of the 2019 Gilded Enigma dues statement and accompanying explanatory information. Over the next couple months, I developed and presented questions and observations to corporate via the Gilded Enigma Parent Company Manager.

<u>February 2019</u>: In pursuing answers to my questions regarding the dues statement, I received the HOA project documents from the Gilded Enigma Manager, which raised even further inquiries. I sent a substantive letter expressing additional areas of concern with questions and observations. Gilded Enigma management began stonewalling.

<u>March 2019</u>: For additional information about the broader timeshare industry, I wrote to the American Resort Development Association (ARDA), requesting a visit. ARDA stonewalling began and continues.

<u>March 28, 2019</u>: I sought to introduce selected ques-

tions still not answered from my 2/2019 letter to the Gilded Enigma HOA 2019 Annual Board Meeting. Chairman disallowed in favor of having a private discussion afterward. I had a private discussion of some length with a senior executive of Parent Company, followed with brief written communication in the following days.

May 2019: I pointed out compliance issues and suggested additional documentation and script to facilitate point of sale at the Gilded Enigma to the senior executive of Parent Company, then to the CEO of the corporation the Parent Company had spun off. Neither responded.

Appendix 2

ACRONYMS USED IN BOOK

ACRONYM	MEANING	COMMENTS
ARDA	American Resort Development Association	Association representing the timeshare industry
ARDA-ROC	American Resort Development Association-Resort Owners Coalition	Part of ARDA representing resort (timeshare) owners
CFPB	Consumer Financial Protection Bureau	Launched in 2011 to protect consumers from financial fraud

GE	Gilded Enigma	Fourth and last time-share purchased by author
MA	Management Agreement	The contract outlining terms and conditions of a timeshare manager
MF	Management Firm	The firm engaged in managing timeshare project(s)
ML	Mountain Lodge	Second timeshare (equity residence club) purchased by author
MM	Midtown Modernity	Third timeshare purchased by the author
OMT	Owner/Member/Tenant	All-encompassing acronym used by author to describe those purchasing timeshares
PPP	Payroll Protection Program	Federal government program to assist small business owners during COVID-19

Appendix 3
BOOK CHARACTERS BY SEQUENCE

NAME	DESCRIPTION	FIRST APPEARANCE
RON	Sales management at MM	Chapter 3, p. 36
ADAM	Dean's boss and senior executive at MF managing many properties, including MM and GE	Chapter 3, p. 43
LUCY	Club director of GE	Chapter 3, p. 43
DEAN	Executive at MF	Chapter 3, p. 49
SPARKY	Timeshare salesman at GE	Chapter 4, p. 74

JIM	Prospective retiree looking for an additional and generous source of retirement income	Chapter 5, p. 81–85
BOB	Beloved and tenured member of Old Guard staff	Chapter 7, p. 100

Appendix 4

RESALE QUESTIONS

Note: nineteen years into my personal experiences with timeshare ownership, I had my first real glimpse into the sausage factory at Midtown Modernity (MM). As both a real estate investor and active financial advisor at the time, I was an unusually informed consumer about many things; the fact that the "Resale Department" serving MM and others functioned very differently than initially advertised spurred my realization that I was a "banquet only" timeshare customer. This series of correspondence was my first substantial written attempts to learn more about these internal business operations, and the response foreshadowed how my additional questions would be addressed.

Friday, October 21, 2016 11:19 AM
To: Bob, Sales Management, Midtown Modernity
CC: Lucy, Midtown Modernity Club Director
From: WHC

Subject: Questions and Feedback/Observations

My name is W.H. Campbell. On April 13, 2016, I purchased interest in a suite at the Midtown Modernity project for the asking price . . . plus closing costs. Of that, 17 percent was paid down and 83 percent paid as part of a "financed" agreement. Title is now held by my trust. Purchase was made to augment existing NYC vacation time owned at the Old Guard. No exchanges are envisioned, as we have ample access to other upscale properties worldwide. We're leaving for one next week.

Questions/Request: Just prior to purchase, I asked the salesperson (and others), "How did you come up with the price?" I never got a good answer, so I'll ask again here. **Apart from determining desired net profit and what the market will bear, what additional factors, if any, went into arriving at this price?** I'm not complaining; just want to be an informed consumer. My purpose is to gain better insight into your business model. Candor would be appreciated. Additionally, for context and perspective, it would be useful to know two things: (1) the average asking price for selected units over time together with the average amount actually paid by purchasers (if different); and (2) assuming it is to be unrecoverable, the average commission paid, as a percentage of sales price, for selected units.

Feedback/Observation: As a financial advisor, I have cautioned others that timeshares, in general, are a waste of money because the heavy up-front "load" and ongoing maintenance fees tend to outweigh benefits. Yet, here I am. This imbalance was recently underscored when I learned of the lowball Midtown Modernity buy-back offer. Now, to be clear, I have neither intention nor desire to sell. But I feel that as part of my fiduciary duty, I must know more about what goes on behind the scenes. Thus, your cooperation and candor would be appreciated.

That said, it's apparent the resale program is another profit center for your company. I have no problem with that, but it begs the question why owners are presented *misinformation* about how to use it. Here's what I mean: When resale questions arise, call center employees are taught to direct owners to the "Resale Department." Makes sense, but here's my experience: To learn more, I left a voice-mail inquiry on 7/29/2016. Having heard nothing by late September, I complained to the call center that the department seems, at best, to be inattentive, or at worst, a sham—and concluded your company had no real interest in helping members with resales. Interestingly, however, my complaint resulted in a call back from the department in early October. After trading several voicemails, our conversation resulted in two areas of further concern: (1) the aforementioned low-ball number (I was told my buy-back offer would be about 25 percent sales price); and (2) the Resale Department is not the correct place to call. Instead, I'm told, it's the "Member Support Department," and members call there only when they've found a pro-spective buyer. As I understand it, a member should call the Resale Department only as a last resort. Thus, I think it important to train call center employees accordingly and incorporate a discussion of the rela-tive illiquidity of these fractional interests during the sales process because of the [blank].

In view of the above and as a final observation on my situation, if the delta between amounts paid and resale value (sales price minus 75 percent) is correct, this buyer has quite a bit of imputed equity, suggesting a great deal of additional value will be delivered by your company over the course of ownership. And with payment of annual maintenance fees, it further suggests any gratuities, et cetera, paid for its use going forward will have been <u>prepaid</u> well in advance.

Action: Please complete the attached chart, address how sales price(s) are determined, provide language to fill in the blank at the end of the third paragraph, and comment as you wish on my observations. Thanks.

With this information, I should have a better understanding of your perspective and more equipped to advise others about it. Should you need anything further or have questions, please let me know. Meanwhile, I'll look forward to your response.

WHC

[Recipient was asked to complete my statement by filling in the blank.]

October 26, 2016 3:42 PM
To: WHC
From: Bob, Sales Management, MM

Summary:

- Thanked me for questions and observations

- Advised that most of requested data was pro-prietary, not for public disclosure

- Imagined that my assumption about rationale for prices was correct with some additional insights

- Asserted there was no difference in asking price and selling price—and that they did not negotiate prices

- Advised that salesperson compensation was paid by seller, not buyer

- Confirmed that the Resale Department was a relatively small office because the expectation was that most new owners bought for a life-time and beyond (for heirs).

- Stated that since it was not always possible for one to keep their ownership for such a long period and that since many owners have neither the time nor knowledge to list their ownership interest themselves or transfer title, et cetera, the Resale Department was created for those purposes.

- Thanked me for suggestion and volunteered to speak to management and trainers about sales staff and call center Resale Department training.

[Recipient was asked to complete my statement by filling in the blank.]

October 26, 2016 10:47 PM
To: Bob, Sales Management, MM
From: WHC

Subject: Questions and Feedback/Observations

In the midst of our current travels, your timely response was most welcome. Thank you for it.

Unfortunately, while it no doubt sailed through compliance, and perhaps because of it, you must have known that it would be received for what it is—largely useless. Sorry you got stuck with this. At least you answered the mail.

It seems the inner workings of the process are as much a mystery to you as Midtown Modernity wishes to make it for me. Proprietary information is another way of saying it's none of your business. I disagree and am disappointed. I'll continue elsewhere.

WHC

Appendix 5
DUES STATEMENT QUESTIONS

Note: although I had every intention of following up on my questions from 2016, my priorities shifted with new opportunities—including upgrading our Midtown Modernity ownership for that of Gilded Enigma. This new building was under the auspices of the company that also owned Midtown Modernity, so I never fully forgot my glimpse into the sausage factory; when I received the 2019 Gilded Enigma dues statement, I was motivated once more to better understand the business behind the obfuscation. After marking up the dues statement, I developed and presented questions and observations to Dean, the Gilded Enigma Manager via Lucy, the GE Club Director.

January 15, 2019
To: Dean, MF Executive
From: WHC

Subject: Questions and Observations for Gilded Enigma Suites Owners Association, Inc.

Together with my spouse, I am a trustee of a trust owning two ownership interests in the Gilded Enigma, now governed by the Suites Owners Association, Inc. (HOA).

As I seek to better understand the business and legal underpinnings of the HOA, I need answers to certain questions about how the operation conducts its business. The purpose is to help me become a more informed advocate and, as a result, better able to make meaningful decisions and constructive input about our "home away from home."

Please help me understand the meaning of these terms used in materials sent:

a. **Condominium Declaration**: Beyond that stated above, what is it? Who creates it and under what authority?

b. **Timeshare Declaration**: Beyond that stated above, what is it? Who creates it and under what authority?

c. **Declaration and Association By-Laws**: Who creates these and under what authority?

d. **Declaration of Covenants, Conditions and Restrictions and Ownership for GE Suites**: What are these and may owners have a copy?

e. **Declarant**: Exactly who or what is it?

f. **Subsidy Agreement**: What is it? Why does it matter? May owners get a copy?

g. **Sponsor**: Who or what is it? How does it fit in with other players?

h. **The Association**: What is it? Am I to assume it's the HOA?

Please address these additional basic questions:

a. What is the purpose of "Club Dues"? Why are they broken out as a separate fee? Wouldn't it be better to simply provide whatever goods and services they convey as a matter of normal business, instead of charging separately?

b. Most developers/HOA creators "adopt" certain boilerplate documents and assume owners will accept them as written. Where are the governing documents for the HOA, and how may owners (through HOA) amend them, if deemed appropriate and/or necessary?

c. Must owners accept the judgment of "Declarant" (whoever that is) if they have reason to disagree?

d. How are initial maintenance fees determined?

e. Is it incomprehensible that maintenance fees may actually go <u>down</u>?

f. Per the budget, to whom are we paying a substantial management fee?

g. When it comes to resources, what is the chain of authority governing HOA administrative (labor) and operational expenses? What comprises the "Condominium Common Expense Allocation"?

h. Why do the footnotes to annual budget say the HOA has "no sources of income"?

i. What is "The Management Agreement" between our HOA and the Gilded Enigma Manager? Who sets the fees shown therein? May owners (the HOA) get a copy?

j. What is a "Brand Services Fee"?

k.   Who is "The Manager"?

l.   Who approves the substantial funds in "Other Expenses"?

m.   Do we really have no control over the enormous sums spent for housekeeping?

n.   What is "The Condominium" and who/what pays it such a substantial sum for operational supplies and service, to include housekeeping, etc.?

o.   How irreversibly are we entangled with existing labor agreements? Why are we so entangled? Can we get out of them? If so, what does it take? What are the consequences? Are owners obliged because others have agreed to them? Are such disclosures made to owners at time of sale in writing? If so, are they reasonably understandable? What rights vis-à-vis the HOA do owners have? From materials provided, I see that certain union contract(s) expire shortly. What options do owners have? Who is really "the boss" when it comes to running the Gilded Enigma Suites Owners Association, Inc.?

p. Who or what determines the sales price of any particular ownership interest at any particular time? Once the "Grantee" pays it, how does your company use the proceeds— and for what purpose? May I assume sales commissions are a major part? If so, and if such sales efforts are key to a purchase, can owners expect similar efforts (for sums already paid) to be made on their behalf (say, after a period of time) to be used for a <u>resale</u>? If ownership interest is a valued entity, assuming property is well-maintained, why are resales always assumed to be of <u>less</u> value? Is it incomprehensible that sales (resale) prices may ever go up?

<u>Here are some observations</u>:

a. The HOA gives me the initial impression of being run "on the cheap." I say that because it seems to treat owners as nothing special, e.g., using non-postage paid return envelopes to collect dues checks (minor but telling), discouraging use of credit cards (seems insane after the sales department insists on their use). As a thought, instead of discouraging credit cards, HOA should give owners a <u>discount</u> for paying by check—especially when it apparently charges owners for using them (see budget).

b.   In your welcoming letter introducing owners to their annual maintenance fee statements, you provide a phone number and say, "If you have any questions regarding your annual statement, please call." That sounds good, but, unfortunately, the person(s) on the other end of that line have no clue. They haven't been trained to respond to likely owner questions about materials sent them.

c.   Finally, I appreciate the phrase used at the bottom of your forwarding letter! I believe it encapsulates the desired result of any effort it might take to have an informed, satisfied, engaged, and committed ownership:

"[W]e look forward to welcoming you back to the familiar comfort of your home away from home."

Friday, February 1, 2019
To: WHC
From: Dean, MF Executive

Subject: Response (Phone Call)

Dean invited me to discuss my January 15 email via voicemail on February 1. I returned his call later that afternoon and took the following notes from our conversation.

The discussion was cordial, but not terribly satisfying. Perhaps the phrase, "It is what it is" best sums up what I heard.

Essentially, we agreed that most of my questions could be answered by information that I should already have. But did I? He mentioned a USB drive that I should have received from the Sales Dept. upon ownership purchase but volunteered to mail one to me. That's good because while I got a nice leather-encased USB from Sales, it had no HOA info on it.

Here were his responses to other questions I jotted down:

He told me what "Club Dues" were, but didn't say why they were broken out as a separate fee.

Maintenance fees are simple math based on costs divided by number and type of ownership contracts.

Always **think of maintenance fees going up, never down,** and rate increase would be about 5 percent per year.

The management fee is paid to Dean himself as Gilded Enigma Manager and others to "manage" our affairs. Not sure it's worth that much to us . . . why this percentage?

The Brand Fee is for our ability to use the Parent Company name. But do we want or need it? Are we required to do so? It seems too high and goes up every year as well. Why must it be this much? How many profit centers must PC and the Gilded Enigma have?

Appendix 6
HOA DOCUMENT QUESTIONS

Note: upon receipt of the promised HOA documents, I had more information to review, but upon that review, I had an even greater number of questions regarding the business operations of the Gilded Enigma. As all my Resale Department and Dues Statement questions had gone unsatisfactorily answered via email and conversations at the club level, I changed tactics and prepared the questions I had regarding the HOA documents with the intention of presenting them during the HOA Board Meeting.

Wednesday, February 13, 2019 5:08 PM
To: Dean, MF Executive
CC: Lucy, GE Club Director
From: WHC

Subject: Contract [Number Redacted] GE

Hi Dean,

Thanks for sending the USB drive via FedEx.

Since I was able to pick one up yesterday from a staff member in NYC, I now have two. As mentioned to her, I did not receive one prior. But you seem certain that I had, assuming systems never fail. Naturally, upon returning home today, I looked anew throughout materials given me at purchase—but found nothing new.

As mentioned to the NYC staff member, a USB drive was given to me, but it had nothing to do with HOA documents. I showed it to her and she confirmed it was unrelated. Thus, for what it's worth, I reaffirm non-receipt of HOA documents at purchase.

That aside, I now have an ample supply and will begin review as time permits over next several days. Thanks for your help and support.

Best regards,
WHC

Monday, February 18, 2019 2:56 PM
To: Dean, MF Executive
CC: Lucy, GE Club Director
From: WHC

Subject: Management Services

Hi Dean,

Greetings to you as we celebrate the birthday of the Father of our Country! Hope you're enjoying some time off.

Thanks again for the documents. I'm finding them quite enlightening, and am starting to develop many questions. So, for starters, I have a basic one: to what extent might I be accruing added expenses for the HOA as I attempt to resolve these and others through you?

Thanks.
WHC

Tuesday, February 19, 2019 1:47 PM
To: WHC
CC: Lucy, GE Club Director
From: Dean, MF Executive

Subject: Response Summary

Dean responded that he was pleased to answer questions to the extent possible and that doing so would not be an additional expense to HOA. He also suggested that should questions require a legal interpretation, I should consider hiring private legal counsel. This was the first significant indication I had of the stonewalling that would characterize all following efforts for additional clarification on every level of the Gilded Enigma and its Parent Company.

Thursday, February 28, 2019 9:20:32 AM
To: Dean, MF Executive
From: WHC

Dear Dean,

Thanks for your willingness to help. I appreciate it.

While having an interest in the timeshare industry and the Gilded Enigma's participation in it, my
immediate focus is on the Gilded Enigma (GE). The
goal is to become reasonably well informed on the
industry, the GE's slice of it, and especially the details
of our newest timeshare interest.

By way of background, I'm a retired naval officer
with an entrepreneurial bent who took up a second
career in financial services as an advisor to the public
on matters of retirement income planning/estate
distribution. During both careers, I continued my
avocation as a residential real estate investor, eventually consolidating holdings in the Washington,
DC, area.

Along the way, we purchased our first timeshare in
Midtown Manhattan about 20 years ago, upgrading
to a Penthouse Suite in 2005. In 2013, we purchased
another timeshare interest, this time in the moun-

tains of western North Carolina. We are very pleased with both and enjoy them often. More recently, we purchased interests in the Midtown Modernity, subsequently upgrading to the GE. As you might surmise, it was our most significant.

Also, as backdrop to our communication, you should know that I'm concerned with what I see as an inherent conflict of interest for the GE's Parent Company (PC) as it attempts to serve both its stockholders and customers (owners) like us. While corporate commentary suggests otherwise, I'm not so sure. Moreover, my opinions expressed in certain "observations" below go beyond documents and may be construed as consumer complaints. If so, others within the GE may wish comment for the record.

While knowing it's necessary, I don't like the overuse of "boilerplate" that comprises most business communication, including language within GE documents. Thus, I'd appreciate responses in writing that are thoughtful and frank. So, let's be real. Because the term "timeshare" is a pejorative in many circles, I want to help remove the stigma. Stated simply, I'd like to make the enterprise of which I consider myself a part better.

Here are my initial questions and observations.

About half relate to the HOA Statement package, while the rest are about the GE Suites Management Agreement (MA). So, here they are:

1. Since I'm planning to attend the 2019 Annual Meeting, can you tell me what time of day it's likely to be scheduled?

2. May I assume that initial Association (HOA) Board Members are GE PC employees? Are they expected to attend the Annual meeting?

3. Regarding a "Brand Services Fee," I suppose it is what it is, but I'm not clear why it exists. As stated in the MA, it covers mandatory programs and services that are deemed beneficial to the project's operations. I get it, but at a property like GE, where owners pay a premium to get in, it seems reasonable to assume such services are a given—without needing to pay an additional fee. Other than being in the documents, what is the justification? Is such provision unique to the GE?

4. Regarding the Subsidy Agreement, it seems to be what the name implies, a Sponsor-subsidy paid

to HOA during a project's early years. Is that it, or is there a potential downside to owners if its termination is ill-timed? If so, can you please elaborate?

5. The documents refer to the most prevalent common area as the "Owner's Lounge," yet a plaque mounted at GE calls it "Member's Lounge." Is there a reason for this? Aside from cost and owner preference, is there any reason why it couldn't be changed to read "Owner's Lounge"?

6. How irreversibly are we entangled with existing labor agreements? Can we get out of them? If so, what does it take, and who would undertake the task? What are the consequences? Disclosure of labor agreements are not made to prospective owners at time of sale, but should be. From materials provided, I see that certain union contract(s) expire shortly. What options do Management Firm (MF)/HOA have with respect terminating or modifying?

7. Regarding my original question about source of sales prices, I see the answer in the documents.

My question now is this: are listed sales prices somewhat analogous to MSRP of a new auto? Of course, this would have been nice to have at time of sale, or beforehand . . .

Observation 7: *If MSRP is a reasonable analogy, there's a dramatic drop in value once driven off the lot! That aside, while the GE PC sales process is no doubt robust and drives the business model, it's notably weak, at least by financial service standards, in one important area with which I became familiar in my most recent career, compliance. For example, there's no attempt at any kind of financial underwriting or consumer risk tolerance, despite the first page of Timeshare Offering screaming of RISK (but what kind of risk?). Yet, if my experience is like others, customers do not see any documents timely. And because documents are not available for review before or during the sale, consumers have no idea until afterward that the quoted "price", like MSRP, is entirely negotiable. Nor do they have any idea of the "Hotel California" effect, to say nothing of illiquidity. If the Timeshare Act and related regulations don't* *require timely disclosure, they should. From my perspective, it's malpractice. So, it's unlikely consumers have reviewed (or been given) documents before the sale, yet the closing process requires them to acknowledge in a "Statement of Understanding" that project documents override anything they may have heard during the sales process. Obviously, the main purpose is to absolve the GE PC of liability, not facilitate an informed buying decision. Finally, I suspect many (if not most) who buy neither understand nor fully comprehend the significance of their decision. For those who may desire it, has the GE considered providing them with an "advocate" during the sales process? Just a thought: as an owner who's been through it a few times, I may be able to help.*

8. Once more, let's consider the world of automobile leases. If one were to imagine a timeshare sales price to be like a "cap cost reduction" provision in leases (after all, I expect most GE profit comes <u>after</u> the sale), why is there no reduction in lease payments (annual maintenance)? It then begs the question originally asked: where,

in general, does the GE PC use the sales proceeds—and for what purpose? While I could speculate on this, I'd rather not. If ownership interest is a valued entity, assuming property is well maintained, why are resales always assumed to be of far <u>less</u> (approaching zero) value? Is it incomprehensible that sales prices (for resale) may ever hold value?

Observation 8: *Of course, all this stirs my interest in the timeshare industry business model, including the GE. This is not to say it's bad—just unduly secretive. I'm perfectly willing to sign whatever non-disclosure the GE PC or others may require. The lack of transparency, cloaked as "proprietary," is troublesome. I'd like to be considered a team member, not an "outsider" whose motives are unknown. Reasonable sunlight and openness are good things, especially if they can promote confidence in the industry. I believe informed owners can be among the GE's most valued assets—strong advocates who, in turn, could become centers of influence. Only then can they state with confidence to others that the business operation is fair and makes sense.*

I'm committed to the GE project and would like to help develop an army of raving fans. Is the GE PC willing to help?

9. Why does the HOA encourage owners to pay maintenance fees by check? How many actually pay that way? In so doing, the HOA gives one the initial impression of being run "on the cheap" on small things.

Observation 9: *Discouraging use of credit cards seems insane after the sales department insists on their use as part of the closing process. Instead of discouraging credit cards, Management Firm/HOA should consider giving owners a* <u>discount</u> *for paying by check, especially when HOA budget includes a substantial allowance for credit card fees.*

10. Why aren't appropriately trained employees available to answer predicable questions about the annual statement package?

Observation 10: *In your welcoming letter introducing owners to their annual maintenance* *fee statements, you provide a phone number with a suggestion that says: "If you have any questions regarding your annual statement, please call." That sounds good but, unfortunately, the person(s) on the other end of the line have no clue. It's not their fault. They just haven't been trained to respond to likely owner questions.*

11. Regarding management authority in the Management Agreement (MA), I see that Management has authority to supervise and direct all phases of advertising, sales, reservations, and business promotion for the project. This seems an odd distraction for a management firm. Is it? Will you please elaborate to help me better understand any benefits that might accrue to owners?

12. Related to delegation and as we discussed by phone, please elaborate on the awkward and costly situation created in the past by the Board wherein they hired and paid an outside contractor (ostensibly to save money) only to be billed a greater amount afterward by the Condominium as a "penalty" for not using them?

13. As stated in the MA and as confirmed in the footnote to the HOA 2019 Annual Budget, the MA has an initial term of five years with an expiration on a certain and specified date. Yet, I seem to recall seeing a new "restart" date somewhere in the documents. Was the footnote in error? If so, will you please confirm the date and term of the current agreement?

14. I see that Management Firm (MF) has the right to "make mandatory Services optional or to make optional Services mandatory..." Does this include maid service under a union contract? Apparently so, as footnotes attached to 2019 annual statement package include an option to reduce housekeeping cleanings to two per week. If owners desire, what does it take to make this happen?

15. The subject of MF's marketing various products, including, without limitation, vacation ownership interests or other real property interests, comes up again. Is this a collateral duty or a significant part the GE PC's sales and marketing pursuits? Apparently, it's the latter. As stated, MF shall be

the exclusive agent for on-site and off-site rental and resales services. Are you self-supervised?

16. Please help me understand this potential special assessment that may be levied in the manner prescribed in the by-laws, including, but not limited to, the collection of an annual fee for lobbying and legislative efforts beneficial to the HOA. Can you provide me with some insight into what kind of lobbying and legislative efforts such an assessment might cover?

17. Regarding bank accounts, can you provide some insight regarding types of account(s) now in use for Reserve Funds? What is the total balance now in reserve?

18. Within those managed properties having over two hundred fifty members, how many (if any) have undertaken self-management? Of those, does MF continue to provide reservation system and exchange services for them?

19. Regarding management fee, there is a specific percentage shown. Can you please clarify

and/or correct my quick calculation from the 2019 budget? It shows Management Fees, which, divided by total expected Association Fees, results in a larger percentage. Is the difference due to the addition of Financial Services and Brand Fees to the Management Fee, making it plural (fee<u>s</u>)?

20. Related to above, Financial Services and Brand Services Fees are not shown on the 2019 Budget. May I assume they're embedded within the Management Fee?

21. The marketing function comes up again, wherein MF may, from time to time, at its sole cost and expense . . . market and sell such products and services as it desires . . . including, without limitation, vacation ownership interests or other property interests in the project. It strikes me this distracts MF from focusing on its primary function, that of management. If so, how does this make sense to our members? If not, apart from being "baked" into the agreement, why must we allow this?

22. It says the HOA delegates to MF the right to enforce all rules and regulations. How does MF do this from afar? And can it do so effectively?

Well, this is a start. Thanks for taking time to review. I look forward to your comments and those of any others who may be involved.

With your consent, other questions/observations may follow related to broader aspects of the Timeshare Offering Plan for the Gilded Enigma Suites, Parts I and II.

I look forward to a strong and mutually beneficial relationship as we seek to strengthen the bonds with and among Gilded Enigma owners while striving to make it the ultimate luxury destination of Gilded Enigma PC.

Sincerely,
WHC

Note: after two weeks, having received no response and with the impending HOA Board Meeting looming, I sent the following email to Lucy, the Club Director, to document and confirm that Dean had received my prior email. In response, while

Lucy could verbally confirm receipt by Dean, she informed me that she was not permitted to sign anything.

March 12, 2019
To: Lucy, GE Club Director
From: WHC

Subject: Statement of Understanding

Whereas W.H. Campbell, owner of two Ownership interests in the Gilded Enigma, has sent an email communication attaching a letter to Dean, MF Executive, on the morning of February 28, 2019 asking certain questions and conveying certain observations; and whereas Dean has neither acknowledged receipt nor responded to a voicemail asking for same; and whereas part of Mr. Campbell's concern, as expressed in the letter, was an apparent "secrecy" with which the Gilded Enigma conducts its business; and, finally whereas the lack of acknowledgement seems to confirm the assertion, this statement of agreement from his representative is sought.

Statement of Agreement:

As noted above and understanding Mr. Campbell's concern that Dean has not received his communication, I hereby agree to send the original to him via approved and secure Gilded Enigma means as I have in the past. Doing so and following up to ensure receipt by him is at Mr. Campbell's request.

Lucy
Club Director, GE

On..

Statement of Agreement:

As noted above and understanding Mr. Campbell's concern that Dean has not received his communication, I hereby confirm that I personally know of his having already received it on or about _____.
Thus, there is no need to send anything further to him at this time.

Lucy
Club Director, GE

Note: ten days after Lucy confirmed Dean's receipt of my February 28 letter, Dean left a voicemail inviting me return his call to discuss the concerns I expressed. He then initiated the series of email exchanges below.

Friday, March 22, 2019 4:16 PM
To: WHC
From: Dean, MF Executive

Subject: GE Suites—Contract [Number Redacted]

Summary:

- Dean advised me that he had tried to call me to discuss letter of February 28, 2019 and said he left a message.

- He asked me to call back at my convenience.

- As aside, he advised me on the scheduled date and time of the GE Suites Board meeting.

- Exact room location had not been determined, but if I called Lucy, she would provide that information.

Friday, March 22, 2019 5:26 PM
To: Dean, MF Executive
CC: Lucy, GE Club Director
From: WHC

Subject: GE Suites—Contract [Number Redacted]

Hi Dean,

Sorry to have missed your call. But it's just as well.

As you should know, I don't wish to discuss the letter by phone.

Instead, as mentioned in my letter, I'd appreciate a response(s) in writing that is thoughtful and frank. If you can't meet the desired timeframe, I understand and can wait. But it's important. I like the Gilded Enigma and am serious about doing what I can to help make it the best it can be.

I look forward to seeing you at the Board Meeting.

WHC

Friday, March 22, 2019 6:05 PM
To: WHC
From: Dean, MF Executive

Subject: GE Suites—Contract [Number Redacted]

Summary:

- Dean stated his desire to help, but before responding in writing, he would like to have a phone conversation to understand the impetus behind my questions.

- Once done, his time spent responding would be more productive.

- He asked if I was willing to have a phone conversation on the following Monday (March 25, 2019).

Friday, March 22, 2019 6:59 PM
To: Dean, MF Executive
CC: Lucy, GE Club Director
From: WHC

Subject: GE Suites – Contract [Number Redacted]

Thanks, Dean. I have no problem with that and should be home between 12:00 PM and 12:30. If that works for you, I'll expect your call then. If not, we can work out something else.

Meanwhile, once composed over the weekend, I hope to send an introductory email on Monday morning to ARDA on the broad topic of timeshares [included in Appendix 9]. I'll bcc you, as it may provide some further insight.

WHC

Monday, March 25, 2019
To: WHC
From: Dean, MF Executive

During resulting phone conversation, Dean and I discussed the background of what prompted my concerns without getting into specifics. It wound up being an amicable and frank conversation about obvious things that were wrong without a discussion of resolution.

Appendix 7
ARDA

Note: as part of my interest in learning of the business of timeshares, I sent this email to American Resort Development Association (ARDA), copying Dean, an MF Executive, for transparency. I never received a response, and my unfruitful follow-up visit is documented in the text.

March 25, 2019
American Resort Development Association
1201 15th St., NW, Suite 400
Washington DC 20005

Sent as Email Attachment

Dear Sir:

I read with interest your recent update, *Large Time-share Exit Companies Oppose Legislation that Protects Consumers*, and found it quite informative.

As the timeshare industry works to oppose the opposition, it further stimulates my interest in helping defend the industry in a serious and responsible way.

Toward that end, I have something in mind and would like to meet with you to discuss.

As background, I'm a retired financial services guy who earned the educational credentials held dear by the profession. I mainly worked in the areas of cash flow modeling, philanthropy, and estate distribution planning. I am also a real estate investor.

Leading up to retirement, I discovered the pleasure of acquiring and enjoying multiple timeshare interests. You might say I was the ideal prospect.

My youngest brother, however, who is also in financial services, has a completely different view of the industry, largely driven by reputation.

This mild family tension inspires me to present timeshares from what I see as a more enlightened perspective, that of documenting the interests of both industry and consumer to make clear something I believe to be true—the industry operates the way it does for good and worthwhile reasons.

But before going further, please don't get me wrong. My experience tells me the industry has plenty of room to improve, even among its biggest players. But this is neither unique to the industry nor irreversible. In my opinion, the improvements are simple—but not easy. However, once achieved, they would go a long way toward improving public image and further increasing sales.

While there are many books on the subject, it seems most on timeshares are decidedly negative. Some are not, but content is usually limited to ways to beat the system, et cetera. And beyond "puff pieces" written by the industry, there are no books of any substance that actually endorse timeshares.

If the facts support it, I propose to change that.

In order to be a "going concern" any business must

first obtain capital to open its doors, and then generate a predictable, positive cash flow from satisfied customers. This is as true of the timeshare industry as any other.

As envisioned, my intent is to present a full story by explaining the timeshare business model, as I understand it, and why it exists. I have my opinion about the model, but players within the industry are reluctant to discuss. Here is where ARDA may be able to provide some clarity.

In the belief that a well-educated consumer is the industry's best customer, it would state the facts in a dispassionate way. And while it would reaffirm the truism of "no free lunch," it would also seek to demonstrate the tremendous upside potential for those properly screened and for whom timeshares are suitable.

In the process, I wish to shed some friendly light on an industry that seems to be an enigma and, as warranted, suggest opportunities for improvement.

I note the pricey membership levels shown on your website. Of course, it confirms that ARDA caters to the industry, not individuals. I understand. Nonetheless, I would like to share some thoughts, from a customer's perspective, in support of that industry —and ARDA may be able to help.

Thus, I propose a meeting with you, your boss, and perhaps other ARDA official(s) to discuss the project and get your feedback. To be fair, I expect to consult with those in the timeshare exit business as well to get their perspective.

Regarding my schedule, I'll be traveling midweek to attend an annual timeshare HOA meeting at my newest and then spending the next two weeks at another.

So, as you check your calendar, allow me to suggest we meet sometime after April 15.

Please let me know. Thanks.

W.H. Campbell

Appendix 8
HOA BOARD MEETING QUESTIONS

Note: although Dean and I were able to connect via phone call on Monday, March 25, 2019, most of the questions I had posed in my February 28, 2019 letter remained unanswered. Just prior to GE's 2019 Annual Meeting, I sought to introduce selected unanswered questions to the meeting, intending to, at least, document these questions for the record. The Chairman disallowed in favor of having a private discussion afterward.

Thursday, March 28, 2019
To: Adam, MF Senior Executive
From: WHC

Subject: Questions for GE HOA 2019 Annual
Meeting

Mr. Chairman (President):
I am W.H. Campbell.
As you may know, I have several unanswered questions and observations . . .
So, pending responses from the Gilded Enigma PC, and if you please, I will submit a few of the questions for the record to the Board for inclusion in the minutes of this meeting.
The Secretary has a copy—and I've taken the liberty of providing copies to members in attendance wanting one.
Thank you.

DISCUSSION ITEMS FOR GILDED ENIGMA HOA 2019 ANNUAL MEETING

(Selected questions from 2/28/2019 letter to Management)

6. Regarding a "Brand Services Fee," about which Management Agreement (MA) says is for "mandatory programs and services deemed beneficial to the Project's operations," I have <u>four</u> questions:

   · Why does it exist?

   · Why must we pay it?

   · Other than being in the documents, what is the justification?

   · Is such provision unique to the Gilded Enigma?

7. Regarding existing labor agreements, I have <u>six</u> questions:

- How irreversibly are we entangled with them?

- Can we get out of them?

- If so, what does it take?

- Who would undertake the task of exploring options?

- What are the consequences of exercising options?

- Regarding those contract(s) expiring, what options do we have with respect terminating or modifying?

8. Regarding management authority, the Gilded Enigma Management has authority to supervise and direct <u>all</u> phases of advertising, sales, reservations and business promotion for the project. Because this seems an odd distraction for a management firm, I have <u>two</u> questions:

- Do you agree it's a distraction?

- Will you please elaborate to help us understand the benefits to owners?

9. As stated in the MA and as confirmed in the footnote to the Annual Budget, the MA has an initial term of five years with an expiration of a certain and specified date. Yet, I seem to recall seeing a new "restart" date somewhere in the documents. Thus, I have <u>two</u> questions:

- Was the footnote in error?

- If so, what is the start date and term of the current agreement?

10. Regarding the Gilded Enigma marketing various products . . . including, without limitation, vacation ownership interests or other real property interests and your being the exclusive agent for on-site and off-site rental and resale services, I have <u>four</u> questions:

- Do you agree that this is a significant departure from management services?

- If not, why not?

- Why should we allow it?

- With respect to sales and marketing activities, are you self-supervised?

11. Regarding the "potential special assessment" that may be levied in the manner prescribed in the by-laws, including, but not limited to the collection of an annual fee for lobbying and legislative efforts beneficial to the HOA, I have <u>two</u> questions:

- What kind of lobbying and legislative efforts might such an assessment cover?

- How is this beneficial to owners—and not just the Gilded Enigma PC?

12. Within those Gilded Enigma PC-managed properties having 250 members or more, I have <u>two</u> questions:

- How many (if any) have undertaken self-management?

- Of those, does the Gilded Enigma PC continue to provide reservation system and exchange services for them?

13. Regarding the Management Fee, there is a specific percentage shown, but when dividing Management Fees by total expected Association Fees, a different figure presents.

   This leads to <u>two</u> questions:

   - Is the difference due to the addition of other fees (Financial Services and Brand Services) to the management fee?

   - If so, are we to understand the total management fees (plural) are the larger percentage?

14. The marketing function, wherein the Gilded Enigma management may, from time to time, at its sole cost and expense . . . market and sell such products and services as it desires . . . including, without limitation, vacation ownership interests or other property interests in the project strikes me as distracting the Gilded Enigma management

from focusing on its primary function, that of management and leads to <u>three</u> questions:

- It may make sense to Gilded Enigma PC management, but how does it help our members?

- Apart from being "baked" into the agreement, why must we allow this?

- And if we must, why can't we renegotiate the MA to, inter alia, call the Gilded Enigma management by a more fitting name, like Gilded Enigma PC Sales, Marketing & Management?

Note: after the Board Meeting on March 28, 2019, I had a private, face-to-face discussion of some length with Adam, Gilded Enigma PC senior executive. Our discussion was cordial, but unproductive. It was followed by this brief written exchange.

Friday, March 29, 2019 6:22 AM
To: Adam, MF Senior Executive
From: WHC

Subject: Thanks

Hi Adam,

Good morning!
Just wanted to say it was a pleasure meeting you. I think our time together was productive. Thanks for making it so.
But most of all, thanks for the courtesy of your time.
Best wishes for continued success.

WHC

March 29, 2019 9:53 PM
To: WHC
From: Adam, MF Senior Executive

Summary:

- Adam stated that he was experienced, and that without a doubt, I was one of the most interesting owners he has met.

- He was still thinking about my creative take on the timeshare industry.

- He stated for a second time that he hoped I did not get so caught up with what might be that I couldn't love what I had at the Gilded Enigma.

Friday, May 10, 2019 4:52 PM
To: Adam, MF Senior Executive
From: WHC

Hi Adam,

Good afternoon. Thanks again for courtesies extended March 28.

I've often thought about our time together, but have hesitated to write until now.

While our dialogue was cordial and frank, I remain concerned about failing to convey my depth of conviction about improving matters we discussed. Unfortunately, the most memorable points I heard you make (more than once) were that you would not (1) respond in writing to my six-page letter and (2) help me write a book. I get it.

But more concerning were your words as we parted and then repeated the next day. It was the first part that has haunted me since. You wrote, "*I hope you don't get so caught up with what might be that you can't love what you have at the Gilded Enigma.*"

It's not what "might be." Rather, it's what must be or at least what should be.

As discussed, an area of particular concern is

one for which you seem to have little responsibility (although documents suggest otherwise): the sales process. As measured against project documents, there are many inconsistences now practiced. They're done for expedience, but shortcuts taken to make for easier sales place consumers at peril. Of course, this is not unique to the Gilded Enigma.

This brings to mind that great enigma—the timeshare industry itself, which has sometimes been defined by critics as a "legal scam." Here, they may be referring in part to such practices as Gilded Enigma PC using the "Statement of Understanding of Vacation Ownership Interest" at closing, through which consumers are asked to do the incongruous: confirm in writing that they are well-informed purchasers when, in fact, they are usually not.

That aside, I write today as a courtesy to let you know that I'll continue to work, as I'm able, through others on ways to improve the industry and the Gilded Enigma in general and, in particular, the area of sales. I do so with no ill will, but rather to help eliminate any stigma the above moniker may create for the Gilded Enigma—and especially for those of us who have become loyal Gilded Enigma "owners."

Sales are good, but in the long run, compliant sales

are better. I hope you don't mind my use of "we," but here goes—we can do better!

And, yes, I'll do that while continuing to love what I have at the Gilded Enigma!

Best regards,
WHC

Appendix 9

COMPLIANCE SUGGESTION

Note: Adam did not respond to my last email, but after further consideration, I did draft a suggestion to improve compliance at the point of sale. I first sent it to Adam, but he again did not respond; after revision, I sent it to several other figures in the GE PC structure and beyond. To this day, not one has responded or provided any feedback, nor to my knowledge addressed this issue in their sales process.

Monday, May 13, 2019 6:34 AM
To: Adam, MF Senior Executive
CC: Lucy, GE Club Director
From: WHC

Hi Adam,

Good morning!

Before heading back to NYC this morning, I wanted to get the attached to you. It follows up on my prior.

I believe something as simple as this might suffice to address a concern.

Its use would provide needed disclosure at point of sale. Although some salespeople believe that "everyone knows this," I respectfully disagree. It's a matter of compliance.

As envisioned, it would be an attractive, well-constructed (not just copy paper) piece given to those attending Gilded Enigma PC sales presentations, to include existing owners getting "updates." It would be given to them prior to presentation and available to keep, if desired.

Once reviewed and approved, I suggest NYC as the initial test market.

It would, in my opinion, be a professional, elegant, and responsible solution to a practical problem—that of providing timely, essential consumer information within a normal sales environment.

If the Gilded Enigma PC agrees, I would be happy to work with appropriate sales supervisor(s) in NYC on implementation. Please let me know if you have any questions. Thanks.

Best regards,
WHC

P. S. Here's a suggested script. After usual courtesies, but before starting any fact-finding and/or presentation, sales professionals would say something like this:

"Before getting started, Parent Company [PC] wants you to understand some important aspects of Vacation Ownership Interests. To help with this, we've given you the piece you are now holding. Please take a few minutes to read and let me know afterward if you have any questions. Thanks."

REMAIN SILENT AND INCONSPICUOUS UNTIL CUSTOMER FINISHES READING AND SPEAKS—then address any questions/concerns they may have. When done, proceed with normal presentation. Do not offer opinion or commentary about the piece just read.

IMPORTANT MESSAGE FROM THE GILDED ENIGMA PC

Thanks for attending this sales presentation. We want you to get the most out of it and respect your time. In presenting the many advantages of ownership, our sales professionals may not have time to go over all ownership details. This provides a few of them that our existing owners believe important for you to know and understand as you consider joining them. Please refer to project documents for full details. Thanks again for your interest in the Gilded Enigma PC.

If you opt to purchase, the Purchase Agreement and any loan documents together with the governing documents of the Project contain all the terms and conditions of your ownership. You should not rely upon any oral representations as basis for your purchase.

Prices shown by your sales professional are based on those found in the project documents. However, prices are negotiable.

In addition to purchase price and closing costs, you will pay an annual maintenance fee subject to increase of about 2–3 percent of purchase price. This fee is due at the beginning of the first calendar year and will continue each year for the duration of your ownership interest.

Purchase of a Vacation Ownership Interest should be based on its value as a vacation experience, not as a real estate investment. Generally, there is no established market for resale interests and any resale value is uncertain.

Notwithstanding above, such purchase is considered a real estate interest and you will receive a deed stating your ownership interests. Thus, you will be responsible for paying real estate taxes as part of your annual maintenance fee.

If your purchase is financed with the seller, you will pay an unusually high interest rate to help compensate seller's added risk, as there is no other established market for such notes.

Friday, May 17, 2019 10:54 AM
To: Adam, MF Senior Executive
CC: Lucy, GE Club Director
From: WHC

Subject: Final Thoughts on the Way Forward

Hi Adam,
Good morning!

Having returned from most recent NYC trip, I wanted to update you on things learned from several owners and one sales manager regarding the draft message.

The owners were uniform in their support. In general, they felt it a useful point of reference preceding any sales presentation. Given the environment in which it would be read, some suggested modifying draft to allow consumer to more quickly and easily grasp salient points. That updated version is attached.

The sales manager with whom I spoke read the initial draft out of curiosity and expressed no particular concern, confirming that if it ever came down from corporate, its use could be accommodated.

WHC

IMPORTANT MESSAGE FROM THE GILDED ENIGMA PC

Thanks for attending this sales presentation. We want you to get the most out of it and respect your time. In presenting the many advantages of ownership, our sales professionals may not have time to go over all ownership details. This provides a few of them that our existing owners believe important for you to know and understand as you consider joining them. Please refer to project documents for full details. Thanks again for your interest in the Gilded Enigma PC.

Caveat Emptor: You should not rely upon any oral representations as the basis for your purchase. Instead, you should consult the Purchase Agreement and any loan documents together with the governing documents of the Project which contain all the terms and conditions of your ownership.

Prices Negotiable: Prices shown by your sales professional are based on those found in the project documents. However, they are negotiable.

Ongoing Fee: In addition to purchase price and closing costs, you will pay an annual maintenance fee of about 2 to 3 percent of purchase price. This fee will likely increase over time. It is due at the beginning of the first calendar year and will continue each year for the duration of your ownership interest.

Not a Real Estate Investment: Purchase of a Vacation Ownership Interest is a lifestyle decision. It should be based on its value as a vacation experience, not a real estate investment. This is because, generally, there is no established market for resale interests and any resale value is uncertain. Think of it as illiquid.

Real Estate Taxes: Notwithstanding above, such purchase is considered a real estate interest for which you receive a deed stating such. Hence, you will be responsible for paying real estate taxes as part of your annual maintenance fee.

Financing: If your purchase is financed with the seller, you will pay an unusually high interest rate to help compensate seller's added risk, as there is no other established market for such notes.

Note: after giving Adam nearly a month to respond, on June 11, 2019, I sent the following letter to the CEO of the corporation the Gilded Enigma's Parent Company (PC) spun off from, for which I never received a response.

Tuesday, June 11, 2019
To: CEO
From: WHC

Subject: Improving Operations

Dear Sir:
When I see something that is clearly wrong and affects large numbers of people, I must speak out. This is such a time. Recent experience tells me the Gilded Enigma, Parent Company and, by implication, your corporation itself must improve at least one aspect of its sales practice. I'm writing to explain and propose a solution.

And while this letter addresses a relatively small and fixable issue, it suggests something broader: PC's corporate culture, through the Gilded Enigma, may be unduly influenced by the timeshare industry. This is written because Gilded Enigma senior executives have shown little to no interest in change. Perhaps the following underscores.

As a courtesy, Dean, Gilded Enigma Manager, was copied on my communication to the American Resort Development Association (ARDA) in late March [see Appendix 7]. In it, I speculated on writing a book, inter alia. It was circulated within the Gilded Enigma PC and got to Adam, the senior executive who made a personal declaration to me three days later in NYC. It was at the initial HOA Board meeting where, in no uncertain terms, he vowed he would neither answer my letter sent earlier nor "help [me] write a book." I didn't ask for help and thought his assertion rather odd.

With that, my name is W.H. Campbell. I've been a loyal customer of your corporation since 2007 and an engaged Gilded Enigma PC member since April 2016.

As the Wizard told Dorothy in *The Wizard of Oz* when Toto yanked away the curtain, "Pay no attention to that man behind the curtain . . . I am the great and powerful Oz!" Like her, I've seen behind the curtain—and must act.

As before with the Gilded Enigma, I'm writing to propose an improvement to correct a glaring omission in the sales process, one involving lack of timely disclosure to customers. Correction is needed to adequately serve the public by providing them with a fair and compliant sales presentation with documents.

By way of further explanation, I believe my life experience relevant to the dialogue. After a successful career as a naval officer, I was self-employed for twenty-five years as a life insurance agent and financial advisor, providing cash flow modeling and investment advice for hundreds of retirement income and estate planning clients while under the supervision of multiple private and governmental regulators. As an avocation, I have invested in and managed residential real estate since young adulthood. My ownership interest with your corporation began in 2016 with Midtown Modernity in New York City, and continued as I transferred that interest in January 2017 to the Gilded Enigma. By the way, I love that project and have adopted it as my favorite.

Nonetheless, in reflecting on timeshares and recent experience with PC, I've asked myself questions like who or what, beyond small staffs in state offices, actually supervise and/or regulate the industry? What does the ARDA really do? How much of it is on behalf of consumers (little, I think) as opposed to the industry? With whom do they lobby since, as I understand, the industry is regulated at the state level? If regulation is as weak as suspected, are there any ethical standards?

In affiliating with PC, I was no stranger to the time-share concept, having owned vacation interests elsewhere, including one in Midtown Manhattan since 1997. Upon adding your properties to my portfolio, I became more interested in the business aspects of timeshares and find what I've discovered in the documents to be fascinating.

As with prior timeshares, I've been attracted to them because I liked them, could afford them, and was able to quickly complete the transaction. Despite comments herein, I continue as a satisfied member of all. You might say I was the ideal prospect. I gave no time to any documents. Why, then, am I concerned?

It's because so <u>few</u> are ideal prospects. Even with me, mild concerns started with Midtown Modernity's relatively high acquisition costs, which, in turn, spurred greater interest in the underlying business model.

But the real concerns started in January 2019 and continue to this day. You see, while I had never been particularly interested in documents, I came to realize that I was not alone. In fact, it seems no one else (including management) is very interested, either. So the project documents sit there in the background while business operations flow more or less independent of them. But something is wrong.

And that's because documents are primarily designed to inform and protect the public's interest. When certain provisions are ignored for expedience or short-term business gains to the detriment of the consuming public, something is <u>seriously</u> wrong. Thus, my recommendations are designed to correct one flaw in the sales process to provide essential transparency.

Yes, I've become somewhat of a zealot when it comes to timeshares. As you might surmise, it came about while studying project documents of the Gilded Enigma, especially the Management Agreement. That's when I saw behind the curtain, if you will, and discovered the enormous profitability of them. But are these ill-gained profits? Maybe, but that's debatable.

As I see it, the first "wrong" at your timeshares, like timeshares in general, is lack of candor and disclosure. Beyond that, I believe my total experience, both good and bad, may be of value to other owners and prospective timeshare owners alike as they engage this insular industry which some critics call a "legal scam." More can be provided on that later should there be interest.

But for now, I appeal to your business interest in tightening up the sales process to make it worthy of the PC brand—and a model for the industry to emulate. My suggestions will be a good start.

If important to you or anyone reading this, I'll be traveling from June 18th through July 4th, but will have access to cell and email.

Thanks for your leadership of your corporate brand and for your interest in this opportunity for improvement.

Sincerely,
W.H. Campbell
Enclosures

INTRODUCTION TO PROBLEM
(which probably needs no introduction)

Imagine this . . . you arrived in New York City yesterday, enjoyed an evening on the town, got a refreshing night's sleep in your luxurious suite, then arrived early and excited the next morning to have been invited to hear the presentation—best of all, you'd get some free tickets to a Broadway show just to be there. What's not to like?

You're greeted by friendly staff, and after a wait that seemed long, meet your sales representative. All is cordial, and after some small talk, they begin to present the lifestyle that awaits you if you decide to make this part of your future. And once you have it, no one could ever take it away from you.

It sounded good and seemed relatively simple. All you had to do was pay an up-front fee (your rep was able to get a small discount for you). It was sort of like making a down payment on a home, then paying HOA dues, much like buying one. But instead of buying an entire home, you would only pay for what you want and need. As they said, buying one piece of the pizza instead of the entire pizza (or pizza store) seemed a smart way to buy a vacation "home."

Your rep seems especially good at carving out the best deal for you (probably better than others), getting the maximum club points for monies paid. Although you were told the presentation would only last about an hour and a half, once you learned about the opportunity, you had no problem with taking whatever time might be necessary to secure this deal.

An hour and a half became several hours and eventually, the closing paperwork was ready. You think to yourself, *maybe we can still make the 7:00 performance at Lincoln Center . . .*

When you finally get to closing, it all seemed so blurred. You just wanted to get it done.

In the end, you were congratulated, given a package of the papers, went back to your suite and collapsed. They said something about a rescission provision or period. Whatever, you guess they have to say that, but who cares? You're glad you did it.

The next morning after coffee and breakfast, you take a closer look. After flipping through many documents, one stood out—something called the "Statement of Understanding of Vacation Ownership Interest" (or something similar). Of course, you had initialed and signed where asked, even the part that is now starting to concern you—but in view of everything, you're sure everything is fine and there's no issue . . .

Now, you begin to focus on it, and it says:

> "The Purchase Agreement and loan documents together with the governing documents of the Project contain all the terms and conditions of your ownership . . ."

Of course, you <u>never</u> talked about any of this. After closing, you were given a copy of the purchase agreement and loan documents, even though you don't plan to actually use a loan. But what about the governing documents of the project—what and where are they?

You realize that the only useful and understandable information you got before making a buying decision came from your sales rep—where else would you get it? And you think, *surely, they wouldn't steer us wrong . . .*

But then the Statement of Ownership goes on to the worst part:

> **"You should not rely upon any oral representations as the basis for your purchase."**

So where does that leave us? You think, *what's going on here?*

You then realize you had nothing <u>but</u> ORAL REPRESENTATION to use as basis!

But you still believe your decision was well-founded. After all, you don't want to embarrass yourself or others, so you decide to just let it slide. But then again, you start to speculate over what you missed, like where the governing documents are. Sadly, life takes over, and you never follow up.

Some important points:

> I believe this story should never happen at a Parent Company (PC) presentation. What has happened in this example is not uncommon. It's very serious and an intentional error of omission.
>
> But from the customer's perspective, he has just told the world, and PC has it on record, that by his agreement, he understood and agreed with the "terms and conditions of his ownership." He feels helpless but wants to believe everything is alright.
>
> The kabuki dance starts as all parties begin to play their roles and avoid the topic.

The sales rep and staff are so proud of the customer and his wise decision that he starts to mirror their comportment. Pleasant smiles and happy small talk rule the day—with anything contrary shunned by all.

During this period, the customer is still trying to defend his decision, disinclined to rock the boat by pursuing rescission or even complaining . . .

Because PC has conditioned them to it, most sales reps believe, "Oh, they know all this, what's the big deal?"

I respectfully disagree.

The newbies certainly don't know this! Even existing owners' memories tend to fade over time, as they (and their families) unwittingly continue to be "tenants for life."

Some in management have said the recommendation is totally impractical, going on to say, "There's no way an hour and a half presentation can possibly take the time to cover so much detail." With this, I agree.

The draft **IMPORTANT MESSAGE** is intended to inform and/or remind customers upfront of essential characteristics of timeshares, at least within PC, and to do so without unduly disrupting the sales rhythm.

As a one-page document, customers can read and understand it in just a few minutes.

Should it, as some might contend, threaten to "kill the deal," that's actually a good aspect.

If the sales rep sees customer concern, they can courteously flesh it out immediately and perhaps save everyone's time.

Afterward, the rep either goes on with presentation or courteously ends it. Either way would be a perfectly fine outcome, one that would be fair, open, and honest.

If done right, I contend such action would increase sales, certainly in the long-term, because it's the right thing to do and part of being professional.

IMPORTANT MESSAGE

Thanks for attending this sales presentation. We want you to get the most out of it and respect your time. In presenting the many advantages of ownership, our sales professionals may not have time to go over all ownership details. This provides a few of them that our existing owners believe important for you to know and understand as you consider joining them. Please refer to project documents for full details. Thanks again for your interest.

Caveat Emptor: You should not rely upon any oral representations as the basis for your purchase. Instead, you should consult the Purchase Agreement and any loan documents together with the governing documents of the Project which contain all the terms and conditions of your ownership.

Prices Negotiable: Prices shown by your sales professional are based on those found in the project documents. However, they are negotiable.

Ongoing Fee: In addition to purchase price and closing costs, you will pay an annual maintenance fee of about 2-3 percent of purchase price. This fee will likely increase over time. It is due at the beginning of the first calendar year and will continue each year for the duration of your ownership interest.

Not a Real Estate Investment: Purchase of a Vacation Ownership Interest is a lifestyle decision. It should be based on its value as a vacation experience, not a real estate investment. This is because, generally, there is no established market for resale interests and any resale value is uncertain. Think of it as illiquid.

Real Estate Taxes: Notwithstanding above, such purchase is considered a real estate interest for which you receive a deed stating such. Hence, you will be responsible for paying real estate taxes as part of your annual maintenance fee.

Financing: If your purchase is financed with the seller, you will pay an unusually high interest rate to help compensate seller's added risk as there is no other established market for such notes.

Note: this was the final significant letter I wrote on the subject, which I sent to the President, CEO, and Director of the corporation from which the GE PC had spun off, for which I received no response.

September 25, 2019

Re: Improving Operations (Sent via Certified Mail)

Dear Sir:
Please refer to my letter of June 11, 2019.

While disappointed at your silence, it's not surprising given the timeshare industry (TI) modus operandi.

In today's political climate, there's much talk about socialism. But, like you, I'm more aligned with capitalism, where government has a limited role and promotes free and open markets. It works in the best interest of everyone—provided markets are fair to all parties.

In theory, business fairness implies buyers and sellers not only act in their own interests, they each have access to relevant facts bearing on the transaction. But in any relationship, where one party has significant power over the other, fairness is often replaced with intimidation.

Sadly, such is the case with TI. By its actions, it largely ignores fairness in favor of something like a P.T. Barnum model, where a seller feels free to determine when and how consumers have access to relevant information.

Underscoring the above, while trying to improve the Gilded Enigma PC's sales operation over the last several months, I've been subjected to a great deal of stonewalling. As a result, I've come to the conclusion that like others involved with questionable business practices, TI is engaged in intellectual dishonesty. Experience tells me it's part of an implicit business plan. With that, here are some observations.

PC knows better and has simply chosen to block it out as part of corporate culture. It seems to falsely assume that "everyone knows" the nature of TI (an enigma at best) and thereby assumes it's dealing with informed and educated consumers, justifying current sales practices as both acceptable and ethical. But they aren't, so where's the supervision?

Through extensive and costly lobbying efforts by the ARDA and its allies, PC, inter alia, coupled with what seems to be compromised legal counsel, TI has engineered itself to be self-regulated. When coupled with a lack of candor, it's actually non-regulated, despite a well-protected facade suggesting otherwise. Frankly, it's in serious need of supervision.

Having no essential up-front disclosure and no easily discernible rescission procedures, together with no ongoing "watchdog" to look out for their interests, consumers are left to complain to developers in hopes of getting a meaningful response—but they're ignored. This, too, seems to be baked into the business plan. Oh yes, if able to engage an intermediary, they're given plenty of "happy talk" to help assuage concerns and make them feel as if they have a friend. But they don't—just the opposite.

From my perspective, it's all part of a richly choreographed (but unnecessary) canard. In addition, the timeshare resale and/or exit industry, claiming the role of consumer champion, is more a part of the problem, not the solution. So, from my observation, both are rigged against consumers. But they shouldn't be.

You see, timeshares can be <u>good</u> for the right customer. I should know. Apart from the obvious quick profit motive, why make something that's good so dark and deceptive?

At one point, I had naively expected your corporation and PC to rise above this insidious "group think" by at least taking one of my simple suggestions for improvement seriously. I was wrong.

Meanwhile, I will continue to speak out and search for solutions to jolt the industry out of its complacency—and, perhaps, inject a needed dose of integrity. Through it all, I believe TI can survive and thrive.

Sincerely,
W.H. Campbell

Appendix 10
SIMPLIFIED GLOSSARY OF TIMESHARE TERMS

Note: I wish I could provide you with redacted examples of the various documents I received as a timeshare OMT that spurred so many of my questions and concerns: the annual statements, HOA documents, budgets, et cetera. However, legal counsel advised against it. I believe every prospective timeshare OMT should fully review these documents for any timeshare purchase they are considering and have the opportunity to have their own questions and concerns addressed prior to purchase. As I did not have the opportunity to fully review these documents prior to purchase, I am still working to have my own questions and concerns addressed. I have put together this simplified glossary of the terms I have asked questions or raised concerns about, along with any answers I have received or gleaned from my own timeshare interests. Although other timeshares may have different terms, I include these definitions here in the hopes they can help you find your own answers for the purchase you are interested in making. Do not rely on the definitions I have found to inform your purchase; consult the project documents of the timeshare you are considering and experts in the field for the legal definitions you require.

Consult project documents for legal definitions.

Association: A group encompassing all OMTs of a timeshare project who are represented by a Board of Directors in coordination with, as appropriate, a hired professional manger to manage the project.

Association Fees: See *Maintenance Fees.* It's the periodic payments OMTs make to pay all costs of operating the timeshare, including contributions to a reserve fund for future expenses.

Brand Services Fee: The fee paid by OMTs of some timeshare projects for the timeshare to be granted the right to use a parent corporation's name. This will not apply to every timeshare project but can be expected for those that have recognizable names attached—e.g., Disney, Hilton, Hyatt, et cetera.

Cap Cost Reduction: This is short for "capitalized cost reduction" which has nothing to do with timeshares but is used in the book as an analogy to compare the purchase of a timeshare with that of leasing an automobile, whereby one may reduce the cost of financing with an upfront payment.

Club Dues: Such dues are the means for paying the costs and expenses of a particular timeshare. OMTs are responsible for paying these in the manner prescribed by project by-laws.

Condominium Common Expense Allocation: These are funds allocated for the repair or replacement of the timeshare. These include such things as any charges against the timeshare as a whole, the cost of casualty, flood, and/or liability insurance on the physical property, as well as insurance coverage relating to the interior of any suite owned by the Association and the common areas.

Condominium Declaration: The document that "declares" the existence of a timeshare project. It's part of the "Project Documents."

It's the fundamental document created by the sponsor (usually the developer) that establishes a timeshare project. Specifically, it's a legal document filed in the county or state in which the timeshare project will be located. Once filed with the appropriate public official, it establishes the existence of the project and divides it into layers of ownership. It includes legal descriptions of the condominium and each individual unit, the nature and scope of the development, and several provisions regarding the use of its units and common areas.

Declarant: The person or entity (usually the developer) declaring the existence of a timeshare project and the "Project Documents" that create it.

Declaration and Association By-Laws: The document that "declares" the existence of specific by-laws by which a timeshare project will be run. It's part of the "Project Documents."

By-Laws govern how the property will be maintained and used by both owners and the management company, as applicable. They are created and declared by the sponsor (usually the developer) and then, once the project is out of developer control, maintained and revised as needed by the Board of Directors.

Declaration of Covenants, Conditions and Restrictions: See *Timeshare Declaration*. It's part of the "Project Documents."

These create and govern the rights of owners of timeshare properties.

Financial Services Fee: Generally, this is a fee charged in Association books against OMTs' use of financial services to pay various fees (maintenance fees, et cetera) by credit card or other means that costs them extra money. Ironically, this fee is assessed to all OMTs to "reimburse" the Association (usually the timeshare developer) for the cost.

Labor Agreements: It's a contract between labor and management governing wages and benefits together with working conditions. When affecting timeshares, such unionized collective bargaining agreements reduce the flexibility of management to control costs. Essentially, it guarantees the timeshare project must use union labor.

Management Agreement: It's the formalized agreement between a timeshare Association and a management firm, often imposed on the Association by the developer, which spells out the terms and conditions under which they operate.

Management Fee: This is how the management firm (and its manager) is paid. It's usually a percentage of total maintenance fees paid by Association OMTs. This can be a surprisingly large expense and should be watched closely by the Board of Directors. Like the Management Agreement, it's often imposed on an Association by the developer. It can be 10 percent or higher of total Association receipts.

Management Firm/Manager: For practical purposes, the management firm and manager are the same. Both are typically a part of the developer's organization and usually thought of as one.

Maintenance Fees: See *Association Fees*. These are the fees that pay for everything in the Association, which means, essentially, they pay for everything in the timeshare.

OMT: All-encompassing acronym ("Owner/ Member/Tenant") I use to describe those purchasing timeshares.

Other Expenses: All expenses that are not otherwise delineated in the project documents.

Potential Special Assessment: Such assessments may be used to pay hard to predict, emergent timeshare costs, those beyond the capacity of operating expenses and accumulated reserve funds to satisfy. See project documents for use. If called upon by the Association (often the developer) it will require an additional (special) outlay by OMTs. These are generally rare.

Reserve Funds: These are not rare. They are funds set aside to pay for known and reasonably predictable timeshare capital expenses that will occur sometime in the future. Contributions come from normal maintenance fees and are part of the Association's budget. Unlike funds that may be needed as part of a special assessment, reserve funds are planned in advance and are based on a formalized reserve fund study. To remain current, the study should be periodically reviewed and updated as needed.

Sponsor: This term is often used and considered synonymous with the terms "Developer" and "Declarant." This person or entity is the locomotive that funds a timeshare project.

Statement of Understanding: In general, this refers to a concluding clause in a contract in which the parties assert their understanding of certain terms within the contract. See below commentary found elsewhere in the book.

With respect to timeshares, many statements of understanding include wording that goes something like this: the consumer (the very reason for the industry's success) understands (well after making a purchase decision) that their decision is based solely on the purchase agreement and loan documents together with the governing documents of the project, which (they're advised) contain all the terms and conditions of their ownership—*and that they should not rely upon any oral presentations as the basis for their purchase.*

But in many cases, I contend, that's simply not true: consumers are required to attest to this in writing at closing, well <u>after</u> they've made their buying decision and well <u>before</u> they are able to see (if ever) the documents upon which, it's assumed, they've based their decision. Thus, as a practical matter, consumers have <u>no</u> basis upon which to make their decision <u>except</u> for an oral presentation. The creation of this scurrilous "evidence" to the contrary is particularly egregious.

Subsidy Agreement: This is usually a short-term but renewable agreement between the Declarant (usually the developer) and the applicable Association (the OMTs), the purpose of which is to help keep the Association solvent during a timeshare project's early year(s).

In such documents, the Declarant is obligated to pay the Association the assessments (maintenance fees) levied against its unsold units or, in lieu thereof, to make "subsidy" payments to the Association.

Timeshare Declaration: The document that "declares" how the timeshare project will be run. It's part of the "Project Documents."

It's actually the Declaration of Covenants, Conditions and Restrictions & Ownership Interests, commonly referred to as HOA CCRC's. It's the document recorded in the real estate records of the applicable municipality or government office where a timeshare is located. The purpose is to create and govern the rights of owners of timeshare properties. It is created by the sponsor (developer).